The Official
PATROL
LEADER
HANDBOOK

of the

BOY SCOUTS OF AMERICA

With contributions by

William "Green Bar Bill" Hillcourt

and Keith Monroe

CONTENTS

Part 1 BEING A PATROL LEADER

Chapter

1. Welcome to Scouting's Toughest Job   6-9

2. Patrol Spirit   10-34
   Together, 10-14; The Baden-Powell Patrol, 15-21; Solving Problems, 22-34

3. The Patrol and the Troop   35-57
   The Patrol Leaders' Council, 36-37; Meetings of the Patrol Leaders' Council, 38-41; Follow Up, 41-42; The Patrol at Troop Activities, 42-43; The Patrol at Troop Meetings, 43-45; The Patrol on Troop Hikes, 46; The Patrol in Short-Term Camps, 47; The Patrol at Other Troop Activities, 47; The Patrol in Troop Summer Camp, 48; The Order of the Arrow, 49-50; You and the Other Troop Leaders, 50-53; Scoutmasters Are Different, 54-57

4. Successful Patrol Meetings   58-83
   Where? 59; When? 59; What? 60; How? 61; Ideas for Successful Patrol Meetings, 62-71; Patrol Meeting Games, 72-83

5. Happy Hiking   84-105
   Planning Your Patrol Hike, 86-88; Hints for the Trail, 88-93; Many Kinds of Hikes, 93-97; Danger! 97-99; It's Funny About Hardships, 99-100; Hiking Cadences, 100-01; Patrol Hike Games, 102-05

6. Camping Is Where the Fun Is   106-25
   Camp Planning, 108; Taking Off, 110-11; Getting There, 111-12; Menus Make a Difference, 112-14; Activities in Camp, 114; Rules for a Safe Camp, 114-16; Campfires, 116-18; Will You Be Welcomed Back? 118-19; Patrol Camp Games, 120-25

7. Advancement   126-43
   Onward to First Class, 126; Scout Skills—Earning
   Skill Awards, 127; Hints for Required Skill Awards,
   128-35; Hints for Nonrequired Skill Awards, 136-41;
   Scout Participation—Scout Spirit, 142; The Final
   Steps, 143

8. Exit Smiling   144-46
   When You Felt Like Quitting, 144-45; Sometimes
   You're a Hero, 145-46; The Dividends Keep Coming,
   146; What's Next? 146

Part 2 TOOLS FOR YOUR JOB

Games and Activities   148-69
   Fitness, 148-57; Compass, 157-61; Measurement,
   162; Communication, 163-65; Observation, 166;
   Stalking, 166-67; Camping, 168-69

Patrol Menus   170-77
   Hike and Trail Foods, 171; Patrol Menu No. 1, 172;
   Patrol Menu No. 2, 174; Patrol Menu No. 3, 176

Campfires   178-86
   Songs, 178; Yells, 178-80; Hand Claps, 180-81;
   Catch-on Games, 181-82; Skits, 183; Shorties, 183-
   85; Storytelling, 186

Projects   186-99
   Your Flying Colors, 187-91; Build a Flag Stand, 191;
   A Patrol Chest, 192; Adaptable Patrol Corners, 193-
   94; Patrol Food Chest, 195-97; Strategy With Stars or
   Something (Wall Chart), 198; Baden-Powell Patrol
   Requirements, 199

Index   200-04

A MESSAGE FROM THE CHIEF

A hearty salute to all who have been elected for leadership responsibilities in a patrol!

It is a special opportunity to learn and grow in leadership abilities and teamwork. You can really help your patrol and troop in meetings, activities, and outdoor adventures.

This book is a good guide in planning and making decisions to help you as a leader. Your patrol depends upon you for action and good leadership.

You have my best wishes in this important effort and our prayers to help you succeed as a leader in the Boy Scouts of America.

Sincerely,

J L Tarr

J.L. Tarr
Chief Scout Executive

Part 1

BEING A PATROL LEADER

Chapter 1

Welcome to Scouting's Toughest Job

Hurray for you! Some of the Scouts and the leaders of your troop have found you worthy of becoming a patrol leader. You have shown them the kind of Scout you are. You have proved that you have the ability to lead a small group of Scouts into the adventure of Scouting!

More power to you!

There are exciting days ahead of you and the Scouts in your patrol. There'll be plenty of adventure, work, and play—and plenty of one of the finest things in the world: comradeship.

Get all the fun you can out of being a patrol leader! But remember there's much more to it than that. Your greatest thrill as a leader will be your chance to turn a group of boys into a real Scout patrol, to help five or six or seven ordinary boys become good Scouts.

THE TOUGHEST JOB. Patrol leadership has been described as "Scouting's toughest job." Why? Because this is where a leader has direct contact with boys. This is where a leader has the greatest opportunity to influence the boys in his care, to do more than anybody else can do to give them a chance to share in that better life we call SCOUTING!

The tough part about this job is its importance. It's a lot like the quarterback on a football team. No one gets that job unless he's pretty good—and tough. Your patrol members are looking to you to call the plays.

On becoming a patrol leader you joined a special company. Scouting, here in the United States and around the world, recognizes you and other patrol leaders as the spark plugs of the movement. You make it go.

If there were no patrol leaders, there would be no Scouting. Right from the beginning, troops were led by patrol leaders with the guidance of Scoutmasters.

However, making the jump from Boy Scout to patrol leader takes a lot of effort, but this book will help you. In it you will find ideas that worked for other patrol leaders. And you are not alone. Your Scoutmaster and senior patrol leader and parents will help—patrol members will, too, if you ask. Being a patrol leader takes more planning than you've ever done before, maybe. But you can learn how, and do the job. Many thousands have—and learned leadership that they used all their lives.

Every one of your Scouts will have a part to play in making the patrol whatever it turns out to be. But the biggest responsibility is yours. Your leadership, your friendliness, your enthusiasm, your example will count the most.

Under the right kind of leader almost any small group of Scouts can become a real patrol. So, Mr. Patrol Leader, it's up to you to get straight to the heart of your job and then set out on the right track.

Your *Boy Scout Handbook*. Your *Official Boy Scout Handbook* will show you the way. That *Handbook* has been your guide as YOU moved onward and upward in Scouting. That

Handbook will be your guide as you take on the job of leading the Scouts in your patrol onward and upward.

Open your *Handbook* to page 9. Read carefully what it says. This is what the Boy Scouts of America—the movement to which you belong—promises every boy who becomes a Scout: a chance to have fun hiking and camping with his best friends...to become an outdoorsman, trained to take care of himself in the wilds. But also to help him grow into responsible manhood—ready to stand on his own feet and able "to help other people at all times."

Your job as patrol leader is to make every page of that *Boy Scout Handbook* come alive in the lives of your Scouts.

You do this by giving enthusiastic leadership to your patrol in all troop undertakings: troop meetings, hikes, camps, special projects. And you do it by planning exciting patrol activities with your Scouts and carrying them through to the best of your ability: especially patrol meetings. And, when qualified, you can lead patrol hikes, camps, and other patrol activities.

Set a goal for yourself. Your goal should be to make your patrol as good as you possibly can—the best in the troop. Why? Because by making a good patrol you'll help each boy in it become a good all-around Scout—and you'll become one yourself.

Get the idea of making your patrol the best possible planted firmly in your heart and mind so that it's behind everything you say and do. Then, the first thing you know, your Scouts will feel exactly the same way.

Be their leader, the fellow who points the way—but share your leadership. That's how you'll get every Scout in the patrol eager to do his part in all patrol undertakings. That's how your patrol will become tops.

You and your patrol members are all in the same boat. Yelling orders won't help your crew pull together, but setting a goal they all want to reach and showing them how to get there, will.

Chapter 2

Patrol Spirit

Well, there's the patrol, the whole bunch of Scouts looking to you to lead them into the fun and adventure and comradeship of Scouting.

They are different in size and intelligence and temperament. There aren't two of them alike, yet they have one thing in common with each other and with you: they are Scouts because they want to be and not because anyone told them they had to be!

Now, think for a moment of what the patrol is going to mean to all of you in the future. For 1 year, 2 or perhaps more, your lives will be running along the same trail. You will have the same Scouting interests, the same ambitions for your patrol, the same hopes. Together you will undertake great things, enjoy many adventures, share all the disappointments, triumphs and satisfactions that come to a patrol of Scouts.

Notice that word: TOGETHER. There you have the password for that all-important thing—patrol spirit. It's the key to everything that happens in the patrol, to all you do:

● *Planning things* TOGETHER—dreaming up things, deciding on things to do in the months ahead, determining responsibilities for every Scout in the patrol.

- *Doing things* TOGETHER—your patrol meetings, hikes and camps, your participation in the activities of your troop, working on advancement together to reach First Class, moving forward together toward a Baden-Powell Patrol rating.

- *Having things* TOGETHER—the things that distinguish your patrol from the other patrols in the troop: your patrol name, your flag, your neckerchief slide, your yell and song, your logbook.

- *Making things* TOGETHER—your patrol corner in the troop meeting room, your own patrol den, your own camping equipment.

PLANNING. When it comes to PLANNING things together, these should be your main concerns:

- "We'll plan our patrol program 3 months ahead with activities scheduled along the way.

- "We'll have at least two patrol meetings each month, with every member doing his part.

- "We'll have a monthly outdoor adventure—a hike or an overnight camp, with lots of chances for every Scout to learn real Scouting.

- "We'll take part in all troop activities and in all big district and council events.

- "We'll—each of us—earn a higher rank during the next few months.

- "We'll get the whole patrol into full uniform and keep it that way.

- "We'll strive to earn the Baden-Powell Patrol rating.

- "We'll have an eight-boy patrol as strong in spirit as we can make it."

DOING. Now set out DOING things together: Make all the things you planned come true.

HAVING. In regard to having things together, there are a few things that every patrol should have; patrol flag, neckerchief slide, yell and song, logbook. Let's take a look at each of them:

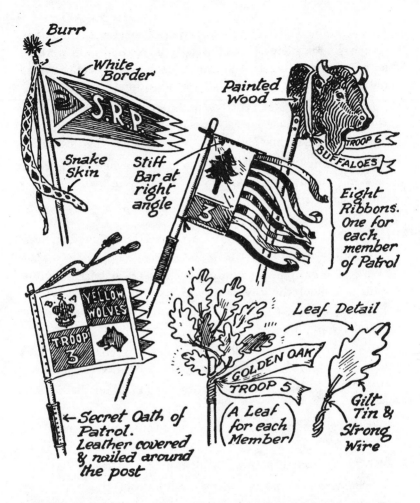

Burr

White Border

S.R.P.

Snake Skin

Stiff Bar at right angle

Painted Wood

TROOP 6

BUFFALOES

Eight Ribbons. One for each member of Patrol

B.S.A YELLOW WOLVES TROOP 3

3

Leaf Detail

GOLDEN OAK TROOP 5

←Secret Oath of Patrol. Leather covered & nailed around the post

(A Leaf for each Member)

Gilt Tin & Strong Wire

Patrol flag. If yours is an old patrol, you're certain to have a flag already with lots of traditions behind it. If you are a new patrol without a name and without a flag, choose your name along the lines suggested in *The Official Boy Scout Handbook* and get going making one. Divide the patrol into buddy teams and challenge each team to come up with a rough sketch. Put the sketches on display and vote for the best. Then put your patrol artist to work painting the flag and get your woodcarvers busy carving the staff for it. For suggestions, see pages 187-91 of this book.

Patrol neckerchief slide. Decide first what it will be—whether it should be carved from wood or cut from leather or whether it should be something entirely different. A Pine Tree Patrol might make its slides from pine cones. A Bull Patrol might cut a cow horn into sections for slides. The trick is to get every Scout in the patrol excited making his own and wearing it with pride.

Patrol yell and patrol song. Get together and come up with ideas for a rousing yell. Pick the best and practice it until you have it letter-perfect. For the song, choose a tune you all like and have the patrol poet write the words. Then practice, practice, practice until you can sing it with real triumph in your voices.

Patrol logbook. As for the patrol logbook for recording your patrol's glorious histroy, get a loose-leaf binder and decorate it to your hearts' content. Then after each hike or camp or other exciting patrol event, have each Scout make a contribution in writing or by artwork.

MAKING. When it comes to MAKING things together, your major project should be to turn your patrol corner or den into a real showplace.

Patrol corner. If your troop meeting room is used by the troop alone, you may be able to put up permanent decorations in your patrol corner.

If the room is used by others, you solve the problem by making a collapsible patrol screen that can be stored between meetings, along the lines shown on page 193.

Patrol den. Eventually you should get a patrol den of your own. Huddle with the patrol and decide how you want to decorate it. Then get to work. The illustrations on pages 192-94 will give you a few suggestions.

Right off, paint the walls and the ceiling in your patrol's favorite colors. Paint a border around the top of the wall, if you like, using a simple design of your patrol animal.

Then build the furniture you need: table and benches, book and display shelves, a stand for your patrol flag (page 191), and a patrol chest you can use for storage in the den and for a cupboard and worktable in camp.

Next, decorate the walls. On one wall you may want to hang the U.S. flag. Maybe a poster with the Scout Oath and Law. Perhaps photographs of your patrol in action. On another wall, put up a patrol "Hall of Fame," consisting of a plywood plaque for each Scout, with his photograph, merit badges, and record in the patrol. On still another wall, you could tack up a topographic map of your area and mark your patrol's campsites and the routes of your hikes.

Dress up your patrol den. Use your imagination, and let the result express the spirit of your patrol.

The Baden-Powell Patrol

For a patrol to have the finest kind of patrol spirit and to be truly efficient, it needs to be a well-organized gang of the right number of Scouts. The right number of Scouts—well, what is the right number?

The more you watch successful patrols in action, the more you realize how right Baden-Powell was when, from the very start of our Scout movement, he advocated eight boys to a patrol.

Why eight? There can be fewer, but here are a number of the reasons for eight:

- It takes eight Scouts to handle the details involved in running a patrol in the most effective manner. With eight to a patrol, each ready to do his part, bigger and better things can be planned. Camping becomes a cinch. Worthwhile projects are easily carried through.
- It takes eight Scouts to make up full-fledged teams for Scoutcraft games and competitions in the troop and for effective Scout skill training and advancement in the patrol.
- It takes a full patrol of eight to present a real challenge to an older, more experienced Scout to make him eager to go on giving his very best as a patrol leader.

So set out to become a Baden-Powell Patrol. Reorganize the patrol and swing into an exciting program that will make the patrol truly efficient.

There are eight steps that a patrol must follow to become a Baden-Powell Patrol.

1. PATROL SPIRIT. Have a patrol flag and rally around it. Put your design on equipment. Use your yell or cheer and patrol call. Keep patrol records up to date. With the right patrol spirit build your patrol up to full strength—eight Scouts.

You'll have extra fun and excitement at patrol activities with a gang of eight. But, also, you'll get added enjoyment out of troop activities when you are able to line up eight Scouts to take part in whatever is on the program.

Your patrol is more certain to come out a winner in your troop's interpatrol games and competitions if you can put up a strong team of eight determined Scouts. Whether it's a message relay game or a tug-of-war contest, you'll be way ahead of a smaller patrol.

And when it comes to putting on a Scoutcrat demonstration at a troop meeting or a campfire entertainment at troop camp, a large patrol is again tops.

The same goes for other troop activities. A full-size patrol is again tops.

2. PATROL MEMBERSHIP. "All for one—one for all." One for all—every fellow with a job to do and a responsibility to carry for the benefit of the whole patrol.

That's where a smart patrol leader goes in for "sharing leadership." This simply means getting somebody else to do something instead of doing it yourself. In "sharing leadership," think of the special abilities of each of your Scouts.

Is somebody in your patrol a natural-born comedian? Get him to plan skits. Encourage him to tell funny stories.

Do you have a cartoonist or a writer? Maybe you could have a patrol newsletter or volunteer to put out the troop newsletter or write and illustrate an invitation to a parents' meeting.

Do you have somebody who likes to cook? Get him to plan something fancy for your next camp-out.

Is someone good with his hands? Perhaps he could make patrol staffs for the tents and dining fly. He could be in charge of teaching lashings. He might become an expert backpacker.

Almost everyone is good at something. Find out what it is. Then try to use everybody's specialties. Give everyone a job. There are seven traditional patrol jobs that you should fill:

Assistant patrol leader leads the patrol when you are not present, and helps you with other patrol business.

Scribe keeps the patrol logbook. Checks attendance at all patrol activities.

Quartermaster takes care of all patrol equipment and keeps an inventory of the equipment.

Treasurer prepares a budget for buying patrol equipment and supplies. Keeps the money records, cooperating with the troop committee treasurer.

Hikemaster plans details of patrol hikes. Cooperates with Scoutmaster in planning troop hikes.

Grubmaster prepares patrol menus and food lists. Obtains food for hikes and overnights.

Cheermaster leads patrol songs, cheers, and yells. Prepares patrol stunts for campfire programs.

Having given out the jobs, now you can get down to work yourself by moving from one Scout to the next and lending a hand. In this way you will be able to keep overall control and see that everything is getting done. At the same time you will be able to work with your Scouts and let them see that you are not afraid of getting your own hands dirty.

Making members glad to work. There may be extra jobs to be done in the patrol. Pick the best qualified Scouts to do them. Tell 'em why! Whenever you ask someone, show that it's important in some way—explain that you asked him because you think he can do an extra-good job at it.

While he's doing the job, and afterward, let him know you're pleased. In fact, it's best to let the whole patrol know. You can even yell, "Hey, look what he did!"

Everyone likes to be appreciated. Everyone likes to know that someone is looking and listening. So be generous with praise and thanks, whenever they are deserved.

3. PATROL MEETINGS. Your patrol meetings provide you and your Scouts with the perfect arrangement for committee work, the practice of Scoutcraft skills, and competition. Dividing the patrol into buddy teams helps to get your patrol moving.

Committee work. From time to time, turn half-patrol teams into committees for coming up with the best possible patrol program of a month's meetings and outdoor expeditions. When each committee has presented its recommendations, they are discussed by the whole patrol. The best features, as voted by the whole gang, make up the patrol's program—and it should be a humdinger.

Or take advanced Scoutcraft, such as pioneering: One half-patrol team lashes together one side of a signal tower, or, in making a single-lock bridge, one team makes one trestle, the other team makes the other. The whole patrol finishes the project.

Games. Numerous games, especially in the physical-fitness line, call for the use of buddy teams: Indian hand wrestling, leg wresting, cockfight, dogfight. Find out who's the patrol "champion" and who's the "champ-nit."

Competitions. Make use of buddy teams in such competitions as water boiling, string burning, knotting.

Buddy teams are of even greater importance when you have your patrol in camp than at other times.

All swimming in Scout camp is done by buddy teams, with each buddy responsible for the other. They swim close together, watch each other, help each other. And when the waterfront man calls "Buddy up!" their hands come up together for the buddy check.

4. HIKES, OUTDOOR ACTIVITIES, AND OTHER

EVENTS. Divide the patrol into two half-patrol teams for efficient patrol camp making, one of them the "tenting crew," the other the "cooking crew."

The minute your patrol arrives on the campsite, everyone gets busy. The tenting crew pitches the tents, prepares the beds, digs the latrine, collects wood for the evening's campfire. The cooking crew builds a fireplace, sets out cooking equipment and food, brings in water and wood and gets the cooking under way.

By the time the camp is in shape, the bull cook pipes up, "Come and get it!"

The same system of half-patrol teams can be used to advantage in a great number of other patrol activities.

Games and competitions. A large number of the patrol games and competitions in this book are based on half-patrol teams. Four to a team means more excitement and fun than if you are working in smaller teams.

5. ADVANCEMENT.

5. ADVANCEMENT. Every Scout patrol should aim toward becoming a first-class patrol. But to be considered first class, it needs to consist of First Class Scouts. A good Scout patrol expects its boys to advance and helps them in their advancement.

But the actual advancement is the responsibility of each individual Scout. No one can do someone else's advancement for him.

The patrol leader's example—YOUR example—is the greatest spur to this advancement. If you move steadily ahead, your boys will follow. It's "Come on!" rather than "Go on!" that counts.

6. GOOD TURNS OR SERVICE PROJECTS.

6. GOOD TURNS OR SERVICE PROJECTS. As leader of your patrol, it is important to see to it that every member has an opportunity to practice our Scout slogan: "Do a Good Turn Daily."

Make sure that your patrol members participate in service projects for the good of your chartered organization, their religious institutions, your school, or your community.

7. UNIFORM. Proper wearing of the Boy Scout uniform is a mark of a good patrol. The uniform is designed for ruggedness and looks good, too. Encourage the Scouts of your patrol in the proper wearing of the uniform.

8. PATROL LEADERS' COUNCIL. You must properly represent your patrol during the patrol leaders' council and participate in its planning and decisionmaking.

Your Scouts will look to you to bring information to them as a result of your participation in patrol leaders' council meetings. You are their representative and they will count upon you.

Solving Problems

What you have read in this book up to now may have struck you as suggesting that the job of being a patrol leader is all sunshine and roses. It isn't. Just like in nature, sometimes a cloud hides the sun, sometimes the night seems awfully dark, sometimes a storm is brewing, sometimes lightning strikes.

It is well to be prepared for any problem that might arise.

Some of the problems may arise out of your own attitudes. Some of them—because all boys are different—will be caused by the boys.

By this time in your life you've probably noticed good leaders and poor leaders all around you. They include your teachers, the heads of student organizations you've been in, Scout leaders, and maybe athletic coaches and team captains, Sunday School teachers, camp counselors, YMCA or Boys' Club leaders, possibly a boss if you've worked for pay.

You've also noticed that you behaved one way with those you felt were "good" leaders, a different way with "poor" leaders. Naturally you liked the good ones better, and you liked yourself much better when you were with them. You could talk more easily with the good leaders, you had more fun and laughs—and you tried harder at whatever their groups were doing.

How were the good leaders different from the poor leaders?

Probably you're not exactly sure. But wasn't it partly how those leaders used their power—how much they bossed you around, how angry they got, how much they punished or threatened?

With the poor leaders, probably you behaved in ways you didn't feel good about. You didn't joke or talk much with them. You didn't try hard to help them. Maybe you watched for chances to put them down, or make them look foolish.

Now, which kind of leader are you? You can tell from the way your patrol acts toward you, can't you?

You can't help your patrol by bullying them, or threatening them, or screaming. If they feel you're too bossy, they'll resist you in one way or another. They'll act just as you acted under poor leaders.

It's no fun being a poor leader. So you'll want to imitate good leaders you've known— teachers, coaches, Scout leaders, whoever they were. What did they do that made you feel good about being in their group?

Of course they all were different. But usually they were pleasant, weren't they? Now and then they probably joked and laughed. They usually seemed enthusiastic. They expected their group to do well.

Maybe you're wondering, "How can I be pleasant when the patrol gives me a bad time? How can I be enthusiastic when they're bored?" The answer may seem strange, but it's true: When you act a certain way, you begin to feel a certain way. In other words, if you want to be pleasant, just *act as if* you felt pleasant. Force yourself to smile.

To feel successful, act successful. If you're not enthusiastic, pretend. Make believe you think your patrol is going to be great. Pretty soon you'll actually feel enthusiastic. So keep trying.

Getting Along With Others

A Scout is friendly. Everyone wants to be liked, but you have undoubtedly discovered that not everyone is likable. It's part of your job to put aside your personal feelings and to have a friendly attitude toward every Scout in the patrol.

The secret of making people like you is to have a genuine interest in others. Become a good listener. Discover what others think, what they like to do. Ask questions—every boy likes to talk about his own favorite subjects.

The voice that wins. How you sound is often more important than what you say. Try to sound pleasant and friendly.

When you talk to adults, do you look at the floor, or mumble? That's bad. It annoys them. Look them in the eye. Speak up clearly.

When you talk to other Scouts, maybe you talk like somebody sawing a board—monotonous, no expression. Put pep in your voice. Gesture a bit. Let your face change expression as you talk. You'll get the idea if you just watch some important guests on TV talk shows.

Two magic words are "please" and "thanks." You can work magic also by saying "we" and "ours" instead of "I" and "mine" whenever possible.

The look on your face is important, too. Make yourself seem cheerful. Act enthusiastic. Watch for chances to say "We're doing great!"

Your patrol will enjoy working if they feel they're working for their own ideas. (But if you insist on your own ideas, they'll leave most of the work to you, too.) You should ask what they think—and listen to what they say—before setting any big goal for the patrol. Let them, not you, choose the goals. Have a discussion and take a vote. And whenever there's a problem, you can say to the patrol, "We've got a problem. I need your advice." They'll often come up with ideas. At least they'll feel it's their problem, not yours.

When your patrol knows that you really listen, really care about them and their ideas, they'll care about you, too. Do you know the story of the Three Musketeers? They were a kind of patrol. Their motto was "One for all, and all for one." Your patrol will get that same spirit, when you yourself have it.

Of course there'll be times when you can't stop for discussion. If you're breaking camp in the middle of a snowstorm, or giving first aid to someone, you'll call the shots. The patrol will expect it. But you can do this in a way that makes your patrol more eager to cooperate. You can say things like, "Joe, would you please untie that pole? ... Thanks .... Mike, could you help me with this? ... Al, we need neckerchiefs to fasten this splint. How about collecting a few from the guys?

On getting mad. Sure the patrol makes you mad sometimes. All patrols are that way. But don't let anger control you. You weren't born with anger. You learned it, because at one time it got what you wanted. As a baby you cried. If that didn't get attention, you screamed. That usually did it. People did things for you, and you felt better. So you formed a habit of getting mad and noisy whenever things didn't go the way you wanted.

Now you're growing up. Or are you? Do you still get mad when you want people to do something? It won't help you now. Patrol leaders who rage and storm don't get results. Their patrol members dodge and work around them, or just laugh at them.

"But I don't plan to get mad, it just happens," you may be thinking. That's true. But remember, if you let yourself act mad, you'll keep on feeling mad, and the patrol may get worse. On the

other hand, if you pretend to be calm and patient, soon you'll feel calm and patient. Best of all, you'll like yourself better. You'll be in charge of yourself, and that's a good feeling.

Here's another odd fact about good leaders, including patrol leaders. Good leaders act almost like ordinary members of the team.

Instead of giving commands, they ask questions and they offer suggestions. They say, "Do you think this would work?" instead of "Here's what you've gotta do." When things go wrong they can say, "Let's try again. I bet we can do better next time."

When to kid yourself. Nobody expects you to be a world-beater all the time. Your patrol will think highly of you for laughing at yourself now and then. For example, if it turns out that you forgot something important, you needn't hide your embarrassment. Gag it up. Drop to the floor and moan, "Former mental giant drops dead," or whatever wisecrack occurs to you. Then get to work solving the problem your mental lapse caused.

If your planned patrol meeting is a flop, admit it afterward. Say something like, "What a happy little experience. I wouldn't have missed that for 5 cents. OK, let's be sure we have a better plan for next time."

But never make fun of a patrol member. It would carry a sting. Always kid them on the upside, not the downside. If someone gives you a good idea, an upside joke would be something like, "Hey, why didn't I think of that? I'm supposed to be the genius in this patrol."

Winning your way against opposition. Sometimes you may feel that everybody is against you. Well, who's actually against you? Some Scouts in your patrol? Or their parents? Or some of the troop officers? There are different ways of turning each into your backers.

First, one general rule: Never, but never, say anything like, "You're wrong about that and I'll prove it."

Nobody likes to be proven wrong. He'll get mad, and look for something else to complain about. Instead of arguing, you'll get better cooperation by asking pleasant questions. Try to convince the other person that you're his friend, and that you want to satisfy him. Agree with as much of what he says as you can.

Let's say you want to get a Scout to come to patrol meetings. You might start by saying, "Gee, Bob, I'm sorry you weren't at the last couple of meetings. We all missed you. Would you come if our meetings were different in some way?"

Maybe he says, "Aw, there's too much playing around. You don't get anything done."

Your first impulse is to snap back, "That's the patrol's fault. I'm not the chief of police. Why don't you help quiet 'em down?" Or you may want to say, "If you're so smart, tell me what to do." But that won't get you anywhere.

If you really want his help and advice, be friendly. You can say, "I know how you feel. It bothers me, too. I'm trying to figure what to do about it, and I need advice. Am I doing something wrong? How can we make this a really good patrol?"

If he does say you're doing something wrong—like yelling too much, or spending too much time gossiping with the assistant patrol leader, or not planning ahead—you should thank him, even if you secretly think it's an unfair criticism. Think about it some more, because he could be right. Anyhow, keep him talking. Ask more questions. He may get so interested he'll decide to come to meetings and help improve them.

Whenever Scouts in your patrol complain or criticize, keep cool. Listen closely. There must be reasons they feel this way. Instead of arguing, make sure you understand, so you can honestly say, "I see what you mean." Then prove it by telling them in *your* words, not theirs, what they've just said. This will put them in a mood to help figure out what to do about it.

Or, if you're still convinced they're wrong, you can say something like, "You've got a good point. But there are points on the other side, too. Here's why I don't want to change." After you've explained, do they really understand what you said? Maybe not. Listen carefully to their answer. Stay friendly. If you need to, explain again, in different words. Gradually misunderstandings will get cleared up, and you can all cooperate.

Keeping the peace. Arguments can arise in any patrol, as on any team—or even in a family. If an argument gets unpleasant, it's bad for the group, so a good leader tries to cool it quickly. This is part of your job in your patrol.

Most trouble in a patrol is just kid stuff. Somebody pushes somebody, or razzes him. You can stop it quickly. Always do this with a smile, even if you're stepping between two angry would-be scufflers. Make their anger seem unimportant. Say something pleasant like "OK, that's enough. Let's get down to business," or "No more wise-guy remarks. Don't you know they're unconstitutional?"

Handling a troublemaker. If there's a really quarrelsome troublemaker in the patrol, be firm. But never put your hands on him, and never scream at him. If necessary, tell him quietly that he's way out of line (although it's better to do this later, in private, if you can.)

If he won't stop acting up, send him home. Of course you can't force him to leave, but he usually will. A hard-core troublemaker who insists on staying and ruining your meeting needn't be a problem more than once. Just tell him, "OK, you've proved you can stop us from having a patrol meeting. But our meeting can go on without you. From now on, find yourself another patrol, because we can't handle you." Then notify the senior patrol leader or the Scoutmaster.

Getting a job done. Friendly pressure is also the key to getting all kinds of work done. Just keep checking on each Scout in a pleasant way.

For example, if the scribe is slow in writing up patrol records, ask him about it every day, or oftener if necessary. When he realizes you'll keep asking until he does the job, he'll decide it's easier to do it than to keep explaining why he hasn't.

Your job is to keep checking on everybody who takes a regular assignment and on everybody with a one-time job like buying food or gathering firewood. Get them to agree on an exact time when they'll complete the job. Shortly before that time, ask them if they've started. If they haven't, ask them again a few minutes later. And again. And again, if need be.

Maybe they start the job but don't get it done on time. Then it's up to you to keep asking, "How're you coming on that job? When do you think you'll finish?"

When everyone knows you'll be asking, the work will get done, and your patrol will run smoother than most.

Correct misunderstandings. Sometimes you may have a disagreement with another patrol leader, or a junior staff member. It could be about an interpatrol contest, or about an idea for camp, or any old thing. Whatever it is, don't make a big fuss about it. Stay friendly. Shut up and listen, until your opponent has said all he wants to say. Can you see his point of view? Be sure about this; until you understand him, he won't want to compromise or cooperate.

When you do understand him, see if he understands you. Explain your point of view slowly and quietly. If he keeps shaking his head, you'll want to yell, "You don't understand!" Instead, say, "I didn't explain it very clearly. Here's what I'm trying to say . . . Now are we on the same wave length?" Whenever two reasonable Scouts understand each other, they usually find a way to satisfy each other.

The knack of saying no. There are times when you must tell your patrol, "No, you can't take that shortcut," or "No, we've got to stay off those rocks," or "No, you can't treat a new member that way."

Take a long time to explain why you're saying no. Give all your reasons, and make sure the Scouts understand them. Say, "Do you see what I mean? Don't you think this rule makes sense?" If they still argue, be firm but sympathetic. "I hate to disappoint you, but

my job as patrol leader is to keep us living up to the rules. If you want to stay in this patrol, stick to the rules. OK?"

When to get tough, and how. If a patrol member breaks some important rule—like bullying a smaller Scout, or stealing or cheating, or throwing rocks, or smoking or drinking or taking drugs—then you've got to take a stand. You can't let it pass, because your patrol will know you're a coward if you do.

Suppose a patrol member, Art, seems to be way off base. Go over the case, slowly, step by step:

- Make sure Art really broke the rule. Who says so? Does Art admit it? If he denies it, what proof is there? Try to give him the benefit of the doubt.

- Was it a rule he didn't know about? If he didn't, explain the rule and ask him to promise to live up to it. Tell him what will happen if he doesn't.

- If Art doesn't like the rule, or feels he can't live up to it for some other reason, listen to him as long as he keeps talking. Try to understand why he feels this way. Then try to show him why he must change if he wants to be in your patrol. Maybe you can convince him.

- If Art won't agree to follow the rule, or breaks it again after promising to live up to it, tell him quietly that he's out of the patrol, and why. Tell him he can transfer to another patrol, if they'll take him. But first, Art will have to explain to the other patrol leader why you can't have him in your patrol.

- Don't spread talk about **Art**. Maybe the shock of getting out will straighten him up. If he wants to stay in the troop, you'll have to explain privately to the Scoutmaster—and maybe to another patrol leader—why Art can't stay in your patrol. But you shouldn't tell anyone else, not even his parents. His family relations are his business, not yours. (Of course, if it's a police matter, or if someone has been harmed, give information to those who have a right to know.)

Parents of Scouts may give you a problem. They don't know you as well as their boys do. So if you hear they're complaining about you, or they're mad about something, this may take longer to straighten out. Here are simple rules that will help:

1. Try to get on friendly terms with all patrol parents. Go out of your way to chat whenever you meet them. If you don't know them, call on the phone and say something like, "I'm your son's patrol leader. I want to have the kind of patrol that parents feel good about. So I hope you'll tell me whatever you like and don't like about our patrol." You can win them over sooner or later if they realize you're doing your best. Ask their advice and they'll warm up. Mothers can show you how to make money go further in shopping for supplies.

2. Expect parents to ask questions. It's a sign they're interested. They may not always understand and may sound as if they are criticizing. That's OK, too. If they criticize, don't argue. If they're halfway right, apologize. Say something like, "Thanks for taking the trouble to tell me. I need to know my mistakes, so I can improve. Can you give me any suggestions about how to do better?"

3. Even if they're completely unfair, or totally wrong about the facts, don't try to defend yourself, at least until they've chewed you out so thoroughly that they've calmed down. Never interrupt. When they run out of words, you can say things like, "I can see why you're upset. Anyone would be. Can you give me more information about it? Why do you think it happened? Are you sure you know the full story? Did it come from several people, or just one person?" And so

on. Keep them talking. They may begin to realize how unfair they sound.

Or they may challenge you, "Well young man, what have you got to say for yourself?" In that case, be extra polite and respectful. Start with something like, "I may be wrong, but this is the way it seemed to me." After you've stated your case, ask: "What do you think I should do now?" Then follow their advice—or else tell the Scoutmaster about the disagreement, and let him decide what to do. But don't worry. Hardly any parents cause trouble for a patrol leader who tries to be friendly.

How to revive interest. Most patrols have one or two Scouts who are beginning to lose interest. They don't show up at meetings regularly. Or they have stopped advancing. Find out what their next steps are on the "Trail to Eagle," then tell them you'd like to help them take those steps. Make them feel that they are needed.

Call them up before a meeting, urge them to come. If they miss a meeting, tell them what's going to happen at the next one. Find out what's bugging them. Maybe you can correct the problem by using the Dean Cromwell treatment. A famous track coach used a special tactic to encourage his team. When one of his stars set a record, he whispered to the runner-up: "You can do that, too. I know you can!" Many times it worked, and Dean Cromwell would have two stars instead of one. Sometimes all it takes to revive interest in a Scout is a word of encouragement.

Chapter 3

The Patrol and the Troop

"I promise to put my patrol before myself, and the troop before my patrol." Patrol leaders make this promise in some troops. It's a simple promise, but a good one. Whether or not you make a special promise as a patrol leader, you should be thinking this way.

The life of your patrol is a very real thing. But no patrol exists for and by itself. In addition to its life as an individual unit, each patrol plays its part in the larger life of the troop.

The troop is the sum of its patrols. A chain is as strong as its weakest link. A troop is as good as its weakest patrol. Your patrol can never have real patrol spirit unless it also has a genuine troop spirit and an eagerness to help the troop make a good showing in devotion to troop ideals, loyalty to troop leaders, in whatever it undertakes.

There are two things that will make this kind of spirit a reality:

- Your own wholehearted help in the leadership of the troop.
- Your patrol's participation in troop activities.

The first involves your membership in the patrol leaders' council. The second deals with your patrol's part in making troop meetings, hikes, camps, and other troop activities successful.

The Patrol Leaders' Council

The moment you took over your patrol you became not just one leader, but two.

You became *the* leader of your patrol. But at the same time, you became *a* leader in your troop, with the duty of sharing in the task of running the troop.

With your patrol leader's badge goes the privilege of being a member of the patrol leaders' council. In this council, you meet with the other patrol leaders—usually once a month—to plan the activities of the troop and to discuss and solve troop problems.

At the council meetings you have a chance to express the hopes and desires of your patrol, to explain what it is doing and what it expects to do. Here, also, you receive the guidance and help you need to conduct your patrol affairs and train your boys.

In the patrol leaders' council you pick up inspiration for making your gang into the best possible patrol. Here you'll discover that by running a good patrol that takes an active and loyal part in the troop's life, you are helping make your whole troop a good troop.

Patrol Leaders' Council
Order of Business

Present: patrol leaders, senior patrol leader, assistant senior patrol leader, scribe, and Scoutmaster.

Call to order	Senior patrol leader
Reading of minutes	Scribe
Patrol leader reports	Patrol leader
	Patrol leader
	Patrol leader
	Patrol leader
Unfinished business	Senior patrol leader
New business	Open
Leader's minute	Scoutmaster
Closing	Senior patrol leader

Meetings of the Patrol Leaders' Council

What goes on in the meetings of the patrol leaders' council? Let's find out. Let's run through a typical meeting.

Who's there? All the patrol leaders and the senior patrol leader are there. Also the assistant senior patrol leader if you have one. The Scoutmaster is present as an adviser and guiding spirit of everything that happens in the troop. At certain meetings, other troop leaders may be present by invitation but without votes. The troop scribe is there to act as secretary.

Opening the meeting. The senior patrol leader is chairman. He calls the meeting to order and takes the roll.

The scribe reads the minutes of the last meeting. They are short, businesslike. Someone moves that the minutes be accepted as read. "All in favor, say 'Aye.'" The "ayes" have it.

The patrol leaders' report. Each patrol leader tells what his patrol has done since the last meeting—what meetings it has held, what service it has rendered, which boys have advanced in Scouting. Everything that shows the progress of that patrol.

Unfinished business. Oh, yes, there are several things under "unfinished." A junior assistant Scoutmaster invited to be present reports that he has secured the services of a nature expert to go hiking with the troop and with any patrol that may want him. An invited member of the leadership corps tells of the success of the collection of books for the Seamen's Institute. Other leaders report on projects that were assigned to them at previous meetings.

Planning for the Month Ahead. "OK," says the senior patrol leader, "now let's look at the month ahead. As you know, the long-term plan we laid at our annual planning weekend calls for the theme of 'Exploration.' So, what are your ideas?"

Immediately, ideas fly about. Every patrol has discussed its suggestions in advance. The patrol leaders bring forward their ideas.

"How about a hike to Mount Paul?" "Naw, we went there the last time." "What about Camp Hemlock?" "Too civilized." "Verona Beach?" "Too overrun." "Chester Valley?" "Buttermilk Falls?"

"Buttermilk Falls, that's good." After some discussion it's Buttermilk Falls. "But not just hike up and back—let's make it rough! Let's go cross-country!"

With that decision, exploration—the troop theme of the month—turns into orienteering. It will motivate all the activities of the troop and every patrol for the whole month ahead. Slowly the program takes shape: Mastering the compass—studying maps—indoor and outdoor games and competitions involving orienteering—

assignment of who's-in-charge-of-what?—getting hike equipment together—deciding on hike menus—making food lists. A whole string of things that will add excitement to every patrol get-together until the big event comes off.

New business. A question of policy has come up. The troop has been asked to sell tickets for a carnival—a request that has to be courteously decided. Another request for Scouts to serve at a church concert. Of course. "Any volunteers?" One of the patrol leaders takes on the job: "Most of my Scouts go to that church."

Other items come up for decision, are ruled on, assigned to somebody to look further into or arrange for.

"Anything else?"

That's where the leader of a patrol with ideas has a chance to speak up.

Do you wish the troop would have more interesting meetings? Do troop hikes or camps need some changes? Would you like more interpatrol competition, or more outdoor games, or more help with advancement? Talk it over with your patrol members in advance of the council meeting, with parents, with junior officers.

Now speak up. Even if an idea isn't the world's brightest, somebody may improve it and use it. You're not much help if you tell the patrol leaders' council, "We ought to have better troop meetings," and stop there. Instead you should say, "My patrol has a couple of ideas we can show at troop meetings," or "My patrol would like to plan a treasure hunt for the troop," or any other offer that can add something new.

Maybe you've dreamed up a good ceremony for the court of honor or a different opening or closing for a troop meeting. Maybe you've heard of a good place for a troop camp or troop swim. You've met someone who could teach Scouts axmanship, or rope spinning, or wilderness survival, or whatever. You've found out that the father of one of your Scouts knows a good campfire story, or a new song, or magic tricks.

Speak up! Your idea may be just what is needed.

Your chances of having your ideas accepted are much better if you don't surprise people with them. Before a meeting, talk your ideas over with several people who will be present. If they like your ideas, great! If not, learn why and see if they are right. But when you know you'll have some support, leadership is much easier.

The Scoutmaster speaks. The senior patrol leader turns to the Scoutmaster to indicate that the meeting has come to an end. The Scoutmaster stands up.

"Well, I think we're on the right track. If the program you've planned comes out half as good as it sounds, it should be a great success. That new patrol of ours is doing fine. Keep up the good work. Let's be sure we have the whole troop in uniform for our next meeting. Well, that's about all for tonight..."

Follow Up

Soon after the meeting, spread the word to patrol members who weren't present. Do it promptly, so they have time to get ready. Make sure they write down the key facts. And make sure they tell their parents, if the parents should know.

Post the information at home so your own family knows. Many families keep a big bulletin board or calendar on a wall, so nobody forgets anything that's planned. You don't want to ask, or have your family ask, "What were those camp dates again? ... Where is the court of honor going to be? What time should we be there?"

The Patrol at Troop Activities

As you've seen, the activities of the troop—all the patrols working together—are decided at the patrol leaders' council, of which you are a full-fledged member.

It's now up to you to communicate the plans and ideas to your patrol, and get everyone behind them.

The plans call for troop meetings, hikes, and camps. They call for special activities for which your patrol needs to train if you expect to make a good showing before the whole troop. They call for high standards of performance, and for steady advancement in every patrol.

Get there first with the most. Whenever a troop is in action (not only at troop meetings, but in camp, on hikes, in service projects or whatever) hustling is important. Hustling keeps everyone keyed up and trying their best. So don't let your patrol lag. Try to be first to line up for assembly, first to pitch in when there's work to be done, first to be ready when an activity is scheduled.

Tell your patrol, "We think we're the best. Let's prove it. Let's be first in everything the troop does. All it takes is keeping alert, and hustling."

Why is this important? Because a patrol needs goals, things to do. When it isn't doing anything it has no leader. You can build up your leadership by setting small goals for the patrol from minute to minute, like jumping into action whenever signals are given, being first to get your tents pitched, first to be ready for inspection, and so on. You'll be surprised how much pride your patrol will feel when it shows how quick and efficient it is. And its example will get other patrols to hustle harder, which is good for the whole troop.

The Patrol at Troop Meeting

Some troops have a weekly night when all the patrols get together. Others meet twice a month. Still others have a monthly meeting of the whole troop, with patrol meetings in the weeks between troop meetings. Whatever schedule is used in your troop, it becomes your duty to see to it that your patrol is there 100 percent. Not just present, but on time and in uniform.

Take pride in having the best turnout of the whole troop. Encourage your Scouts to be snappy and neat in appearance, courteous in manner. Be the first to come to attention when the signal is given, the first to swing into action when a game or a project is called for.

For example, troop meetings usually start with the silent signal for "attention" followed by the "troop line" sign. Is your patrol first to line up? It will be if you're the best patrol leader you can be. Stay alert for every signal or instruction, and push to get your Scouts ready for whatever will happen next.

Color ceremony, inspection, game, patrol corners, closing-up after meeting—it doesn't matter what, your job is to see that all your

Scouts do their part to keep things running smoothly. Your patrol won't always be winning, but it must (1) always be ready, and (2) always do its best.

A good patrol makes sure it never fouls up at a troop activity. It doesn't mess off or play around when it's scheduled to be working on advancement, or cleaning up, or listening to annoucements. A good patrol looks like a team, works like a team, and gets busy when something has to be done. President Teddy Roosevelt, who commanded the Rough Riders before he became president, had a motto that might be a good one for your patrol: "When you play, play hard. When you work, don't play at all."

If any of the activities of the meeting call for advance training, be sure that your boys have trained for the event—at your patrol meeting or on their own. If you have agreed to put on a demonstration, have everything ready to spring into action when your turn comes.

On your feet. A sharp patrol leader almost never sits down during troop meeting. He knows he must show energy and enthusiasm, which is hard to do sitting down. Furthermore, he knows that whenever he's in charge of a patrol discussion, he can hold the patrol's attention better by staying on his feet. If the patrol is sitting down, fine. Then it will be looking up at him. That's what it should be doing, right?

Whenever you run a patrol activity in the troop meeting place, get your back to the wall, so your patrol has to face you and the wall. That way they'll be turning their backs to whatever else is happening, and won't be distracted. "Patrol corners" means the patrol leader is in a corner, with his patrol gathered around facing him and the corner.

By having your patrol ready to take part in everything that goes on, you will be coming close to the standard that your Scoutmaster has a right to expect of you.

Putting on a demonstration. Your patrol can practice a demonstration of some part of first aid (maybe with a doctor or Red

Cross instructor coaching you) until it's good enough to stage for the troop. For example, the 1981 edition of the *First Aid* merit badge pamphlet contains something new that's well worth demonstrating—how to save someone who's choking on food. Does one of your Scouts like to act? Rehearse him so he can give a scary imitation of choking. Then stage a pretended emergency the next time your troop eats together on a hike or at camp. After your patrol "saves" him, explain what you did, and have the whole troop practice it.

A fast-moving demonstration, explanation, and troop practice can be built around almost any Scout skill. A few simple rules will help make it succeed:

- Don't give a lecture. Stage a show—short and lively.

- As you show, tell. Explain what's happening and why.

- After you demonstrate and explain, have all the Scouts try to do what you did. Tell them again, as they do it. Point out any mistakes they're making. Give a loud happy "That's it!" to everybody who does it right.

The Patrol on Troop Hikes

When a troop hike is scheduled, have the whole patrol present at the time agreed upon, properly uniformed, and equipped with everything that's needed to make the hike a success—food, cooking equipment, compass and map, or what not. Let's have no "Gee, I forgot that!" or "I didn't remember." Habitual "forgetters'" are badly trained members of a patrol.

On the hike, see to it that your patrol gets the most out of it. The activities were carefully planned in the patrol leaders' council for the specific purpose of helping each boy become a better Scout. That can't be accomplished unless each fellow throws himself wholeheartedly into everything. That means good discipline, careful listening to instructions, prompt obedience to orders, and speedy action.

On the road, it will be natural for you to keep together as a patrol. But avoid being too "clannish." Mix with the other patrols, if it comes natural to do so. While you are on the trail you often have the best possible chance to exchange ideas and get better acquainted with the other patrol leaders and their Scouts. This leadership business is a real give-and-take.

The Patrol in Short-Term Camps

Most of what has been said about your patrol's participation in troop meetings and hikes fits for the troop overnight camp. It's your responsibility to see to it that your patrol takes its full share in the work and play of the camp, is ready with a song or a stunt for the campfire, is eager to make the most of an instruction period, and prompt in getting its assignments done.

In troop camp, you'll naturally insist on smart dicipline among your Scouts. Your patrol will be the first to "pipe down" after "Taps," the first to get moving when "Reveille" is blown. That will be no problem to you if you have given your patrol a square deal in advance, helped your fellows to a bit of self-discipline, doing the right thing at the right time.

If real patrol spirit has come along with you to camp, you'll have every reason to be proud of the way your patrol fits into the life of the troop. You'll find your Scouts as eager as yourself to have their tents and camp kitchen the neatest at inspection, their Scoutcraft the most effective, their campfire stunts the best acted, their Scout spirit the strongest.

The Patrol at Other Troop Activities

The big thing is to enter into all troop activities.

If the troop is putting on a show, take an active part in it. If a troop service project or community Good Turn is scheduled, do your utmost to make it a success. If there's a job to earn money for the troop, take your share in it—or, even better, do more than just your share. If the troop runs a patrol competition, get in to win!

If you have the idea of team-play loyalty, cooperation with the troop firmly established in your own head and heart, you may be sure your patrol will have it, too. And you'll be on your way toward becoming a REAL Scout patrol.

Your Patrol in Troop Summer Camp

Hikes and short-term camping are great fun. But they really only start to prepare you and your patrol for the best experience as your troop spends a week or more at the council summer camp.

How do you get there? The planning for your patrol begins when the troop makes its plans for the program year. You participate in troop and patrol projects that earn money to make it possible for all Scouts to go. You encourage the Scouts in your patrol to do everything possible for your whole gang to go. A full patrol in camp is one of the best ways to have the best patrol in the troop back at home.

What kind of projects? The troop probably will select the kinds of projects to help Scouts earn money for camp, but you should have some ideas to share when the patrol leaders' council meets to make plans for the troop. Here are some suggestions: spaghetti feeds, pancake breakfasts, bake sales, newspaper collecting, and the sale of other material that can be recycled.

The troop camp savings plan. Encourage your Scouts to use the troop savings plan. Some troops have all kinds of plans and you will use the one of your troop. The important thing is that every Scout in your patrol should save money on a planned basis. It will make a difference: Will one Scout—or your entire patrol—go to camp?

Getting your patrol ready for summer camp. As you look ahead to summer camp, make sure your Scouts are prepared for the experience. Use the short trips to give Scouts an opportunity to practice all of their camping skills. They will need them when camping in the woods for a week or so.

Assist the members of your patrol in deciding what to bring and what not to bring. Use the checklists on pages 65 and 69 of *The Official Boy Scout Handbook*. Make sure that the troop program in camp will meet the needs of the Scouts in the patrol. You can help to answer a lot of questions that parents may have.

And finally, when the big day arrives, make sure that your patrol members arrive at the meeting place on time. Think how great it would be to arrive in camp as a patrol.

Your patrol in camp. You have a great opportunity to help the Scouts in your patrol while in summer camp—a chance to help them grow in Scouting, advance, and have a lot of fun under your leadership.

As their patrol leader you should make sure that your members are fully prepared to take advantage of the advancement opportunities while in camp. Review their advancement progress before you go to camp. Make sure each Scout is familiar with the requirements of a test for which he will attempt to qualify.

For some Scouts, this outing will be their first camping experience. So you need to help them make it a great introduction to camping.

You need to be sure that you lead them well and that you try to help them live up to the Scout Oath and Law. But then that's really what it's all about.

Go to it! Have fun with your gang in camp.

The Order of the Arrow

On the basis of the camping your patrol does with the troop, the troop may elect members of your patrol into membership in the

Order of the Arrow. The Order of the Arrow is a national brotherhood of honor campers and is an official program of the Boy Scouts of America. Membership is attained when elected by fellow Scouts in your troop.

The purpose of the Order of the Arrow is to:

- Recognize those Scouts who best exemplify the Scout Oath and Law in their daily lives.
- Develop and maintain camping spirit.
- Promote Scout camping.
- Give leadership in cheerful service to others.

Arrowmen first fulfill the purposes of the Order of the Arrow in their own patrol and troop before branching out. All Arrowmen want to make sure their patrol and troop have the best Scout campers at any camp.

You and the Other Troop Leaders

In your dual leadership capacity—as *the* leader of your patrol and *a* leader in the troop—you will meet and work with all the other leaders of the troop. You also will, from time to time, meet the people who back the troop—members of the troop committee and of the chartered organization.

Of all these people, the Scoutmaster is the key person. You need to know him well. So read about him on pages 54-57.

He is helped in his work by one or more adult assistant Scoutmasters and by the junior leaders listed on pages 52-53.

YOUR TROOP OFFICERS AND ORGANIZATION

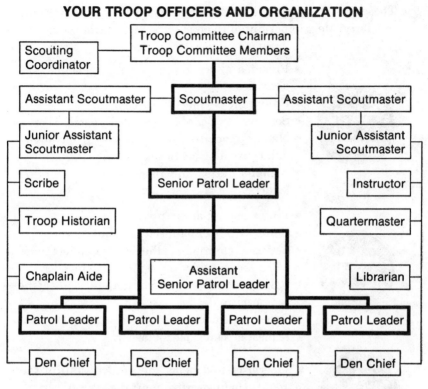

Your troop organization and leaders are shown on this chart. The officers whose titles appear within heavy borders are on the patrol leaders' council.

Den chief. This special kind of troop leader is a member of a Boy Scout patrol but does his work in a Cub Scout pack. If you have one in your patrol, give him all the help you can.

- In the den: he assists the den leader with the meetings, helps Cub Scouts earn achievements, helps Cub Scouts be leaders, sets good example.
- For the troop: the recruiting officer, bringing Cub Scouts into the troop, promotes joint activities.
- Looks to junior assistant Scoutmaster or Webelos den resource person for guidance.

These are the junior leaders with whom you will be working regularly. Most important of them is the senior patrol leader.

- Presides at all troop meetings, events, and activities.
- Chairs the patrol leaders' council.
- Serves as leader of the troop's leadership corps.
- Names appointed boy leaders with the advice and consent of the Scoutmaster.
- Assigns duties and responsibilities to other leaders.

- Trains and guides patrol leaders.
- Helps with leading meetings and activities.
- Serves as chairman of the Scout board of review when requested by the senior patrol leader.
- Takes over troop leadership in the absence of the senior patrol leader.
- Serves as leader of troop's leadership corps at request of senior patrol leader.

- Supervises and helps the support staff of the troop including scribe, quartermaster, librarian, troop historian, instructors, and chaplain aide.
- Works with Cub Scout and Webelos den chiefs.

- Keeps a log of patrol leaders' council decisions.
- Records attendance and dues payments.
- Records advancement in troop records.

- Keeps records of patrol and troop equipment.
- Keeps equipment in good repair.
- Checks out equipment and sees that it is returned in good order.
- Suggests new or replacement items needed to senior patrol leader or patrol leaders' council.

These are junior leaders you may be working with from time to time when their special services are needed.

- Gathers pictures and facts about past activities of the troop and keeps these in permanent forms such as scrapbooks, wall displays, or information files.
- Takes care of troop trophies and keepsakes.
- Keeps information about troop alumni and their doings.
- Helps the chartered organization and the troop leadership in making use of troop historical material.

- Keeps records on literature owned by the troop.
- Advises senior patrol leader or Scoutmaster of new or replacement items needed.
- Has literature available for borrowing at troop meetings.
- Keeps system to check literature in and out.
- Follows up on late returns.
- Keeps the merit badge counselor list.

- A troop may have one or more instructors according to its needs. They instruct in advancement skills according to their abilities.

- Helps in troop program planning to consider religious holidays in planning and include religious observances in activities.
- Assists chaplain in planning and carrying out religious services at troop activities.
- Tells troop members about religious emblem program of their faith and how to earn one.
- Encourages troop members to live up to the ideals of the Scout Oath, Law, and slogan.

Scoutmasters Are Different

Some Scoutmasters have had a lot of experience, others have had none.

Some Scoutmasters can't give much time to Scouting, some can.

If your troop changes Scoutmasters while you are in the troop, you'll see many differences. Expect them. Be ready to change some of your ways to give smooth teamwork to whatever kind of Scoutmaster is in charge.

Remember this: Whatever kind of Scoutmaster you have, he's with the troop because he cares about you and the other Scouts. Being a Scoutmaster is hard work, too—he could be doing other things for his own enjoyment. Help him in every way you can.

How you can help the Scoutmaster. Did you ever think what it means to be a Scoutmaster? Probably you thought it means fun. It does, partly. All the thousands of Scoutmasters are running Scout troops because it gives them a good feeling, somewhere deep down. Nobody pays them for it. Nobody makes them do it. They're with the troop because they like you. They even like the craziest apes in your patrol.

They give up a lot of spare time, spend money out of their own pockets, go off to camp and do all kinds of things that maybe they don't especially enjoy doing. They think it's worthwhile because of you. Not for any other reason. The only reward they may get is that someday they'll see you've become the right kind of man.

Your Scoutmaster wants to see all of you growing up honest, helpful to other people, proud of your country. He wants you to be gentlemen, not slobs. The way to make him enjoy his job is to make him proud of you and your patrol. That's the biggest help you can give.

Smaller ways to help may come up any minute. For example, when your troop is on the trail, is your Scoutmaster plodding along in the dust, lugging the first aid kit and maybe a coil of rope? Could the patrol leaders take those extra loads and trade them back and forth among themselves? When you make camp, could you offer to pitch his tent for him? If your troop cooks by buddies or by patrols, is the Scoutmaster left to cook his own meals? If you offer to bring extra food and cook for him, too, he may or may not accept—but he'll be pleased at your offer, because it shows that you care.

When he arrives at a troop meeting, are his arms full of papers and boxes and assorted gismos for the meeting? Is he busy trying to tack something on the bulletin board, answer questions, open windows, erase the chalkboard, move some chairs, untangle some ropes, set out badges or tools or maps or whatever? Instead of romping with your pals, how about giving him a hand?

A stranger may be at the meeting, but the Scoutmaster may be busy. It's good manners to welcome any visitors immediately. Don't be shy! Introduce yourself to the stranger, and ask if you can help him. If he just wants to watch, find a seat for him. If he needs information, try to get it. If he wants to talk with the Scoutmaster, say, "Let me tell him. I know he'll come over as soon as he can."

If the stranger is a Scout-age boy, giving him a big hello is superimportant. He's probably interested in joining. Don't let him stand there all alone. Even if he already knows one or two Scouts in the troop he'll feel twice as welcome if an older Scout comes up and shakes hands and offers to introduce him to the Scoutmaster.

To sum up, you can be the Scoutmaster's extra eyes, ears, and hands. He's often the last to hear about things that go wrong. The patrol leaders should make it their business to tell him everything they agree he should know. Tip him off to problems, and suggest ways you can help solve them. Sometimes you can even be an extra memory for him. Is he forgetting to do something, or explain something, that you know he thinks is important? He'll be glad if you remind him.

What he needs during a troop activity is mainly every Scout's attention and cooperation. Is there any whispering or scuffling when everyone should be paying attention or following instructions? This is what makes a Scoutmaster feel prickly. Remember, part of a patrol leader's job is to see that all troop officers (junior and adults) are treated with respect. Make sure your patrol members are listening when they should be, and busy when they should be. You needn't whack them to accomplish this. If you let them know what's expected and why it's important, they'll follow your example.

Cooperation with the Scoutmaster is most important at times when he's not there. Maybe he gives instructions that you see no reason for—like staying out of a certain place, for example. As a loyal patrol leader, you'll make sure his instructions are followed, even if you don't understand them. Often they're far more important than you think.

What he looks for in sizing up patrol leaders: How alert are they? Do they see work that needs doing, and do it without being asked? Do they care about their patrol members? Do they set a good example? Do they keep the patrol enthused and smooth-running?

How can he help you? If you lack know-how, he can help you get it. Maybe your patrol's meals in camp would turn a goat's stomach, because you and the patrol don't know much about planning meals, or buying food, or cooking. Then tell the Scoutmaster you need coaching. Probably he'll either coach you himself, or see that you get instruction and advice from the best camp cook available.

The same is true about other Scouting activities. If you're weak in some of them, the Scoutmaster's job is to see to it that you get help to improve. But it's up to you to let him know you want help.

When you have problems in your patrol, the Scoutmaster may see ways to solve them. Sometimes he can talk to parents and get them on your side. Sometimes he can give you ideas you haven't thought of. Sometimes he can transfer one of your Scouts into another patrol, if there's trouble you simply can't straighten out.

Some patrol leaders are shy about talking to their Scoutmaster. They shouldn't be. The Scoutmaster may not seem as jolly as Santa Claus, but he's glad to talk with Scouts whenever he's not busy. He wants to know how you're getting along, what your worries are, how you feel about things. Start a conversation with him as often as you can, just for the sake of getting better acquainted. And whenever there's something you really need to talk over, if you don't find a chance at troop meeting, give him a phone call. He can explain things you don't understand. He can cheer you up when you're down. He can be your combination of guide, coach, adviser, helper, and friend.

Chapter 4

Successful Patrol Meetings

To make all the ambitions you have for your patrol come true, you need to get into a schedule of regular, weekly patrol meetings. One of your main jobs as patrol leader is to make these meetings profitable, to give every Scout in the patrol a chance to gain in Scout skills and Scouting spirit.

The patrol meeting sets the tone for the group. It's here you can generate enthusiasm, where you all really get to know one another. It's here your Scouts pick up pointers that will help them in their advancement. It's here you plan big things for the future and choose the activities you want to share in.

That is, if you have the *right kind* of patrol meetings.

You will have them if you prepare for them—if you find a suitable spot to hold them, settle on the best time for them, line up good programs, and give every boy a chance to do his part.

Where?

Many patrol leaders seem to have the idea that patrol meetings must be held indoors. Why? Scouting is an outdoor game—so why keep your Scouts cooped up indoors unless storm and rain drive you in?

Meeting outdoors. The family of one of your patrol members may have a backyard or a garden corner where you can meet. In a large city, you may find a spot somewhere in the city park. In a small town, you may locate a place on the outskirts where you can meet—where you may even have a chance to practice axmanship, fire building, cooking, and other outdoor skills.

Meeting indoors. To start off, ask your parents to let you have the meetings in your own home. Later, arrange to rotate the meetings among the homes of the other patrol members. In addition to having some place to meet, this arrangement has two other advantages: you get to know the parents of your Scouts, and the parents get to know you and the other members of their son's patrol. The better you know one another, the better the cooperation will be. After each meeting, thank your hosts for the use of their home.

A real patrol will strive to have a meeting place, a den of its own. It may not be much of a place: a small shack, a corner of a garage or a basement, a room in the attic. With such a place, you'll keep your patrol meeting humming with work on the den—building furniture for it, painting it, decorating it, making knot boards and charts and many other things to hang on the walls.

When?

Many patrols meet immediately after school. Others meet early in the evening. Friday may be especially good—there's no homework to do. Or Saturday—although that day is better used for hikes than for meetings.

Take a vote. You probably won't find a time to suit everyone. Let the majority decide.

When you have found the best time for your meetings, stick to that time. Hold your meetings on the same day and same time each week. A set routine will avoid mix-ups. If you have settled on Thursday, your boys will know that Thursday evening is patrol evening. Their parents will know it, and everybody can plan accordingly.

START ON TIME! END ON TIME! Be punctual. Get a reputation among parents and troop leaders of doing things right! That's the way to get their respect.

What?

Five things spell success for a patrol meeting:

- The meeting is planned carefully in advance.
- The things planned are of interest to everyone. The meeting is so much fun and so exciting that your Scouts would rather come to patrol meeting than go baseball-pitching or football-kicking or whatever their other interests are.
- Each part of the meeting is short and snappy, and more things have been planned than actually can be carried out. Not an empty moment! The Scouts should feel that there'll be plenty more things to do next time.
- Every Scout has a definite responsibility in the meeting program and takes an active part in everything.
- The ingredients of the meeting are planned in such a way that the meeting will carry the Scouts forward in Scouting and will help build the patrol into a strong unit.

So what things go into that kind of patrol meeting?

You may have heard the old saying, "Mind your P's and Q's." In running a successful patrol meeting, it's a matter of minding your P's and C's—or, in the opposite order, three C's: Ceremonies, Checking, and Coaching, and three P's: Projects, Plans, and Play. You'll find suggestions for each of these in the pages that follow.

This "clock" gives you the idea of what a patrol meeting should contain. Begin with a ceremony, go around the clock, and end with a ceremony.

How?

You and your assistant patrol leader may be able to plan some excellent meetings. But it's far better to give each Scout a part in the planning and something definite to do.

This is most easily accomplished if you follow the organization plan described in chapter 2. According to this plan, the patrol leader and his assistant run the meeting. The patrol scribe, treasurer, quartermaster, hikemaster, grubmaster, and cheermaster each has a function to perform during the meeting.

OR: If you do not have your organization working yet, try this stunt: Write out on slips of paper ideas for activities that will be used at the next patrol meeting. Throw them in a hat, and let each Scout draw. It then becomes the responsibility of each one to put on, at the meeting, the activity he drew.

OR: Divide the patrol into buddy committees and put each committee in charge of certain parts of the next meeting.

Always start off your patrol meetings with an impressive CEREMONY.

Ideas for Successful Patrol Meetings

Ceremony for opening. Get the meeting off to an impressive start. Make everyone feel that now's the time to get down to business. Take your choice of one of these:

- Line up the patrol facing the flag of the United States hanging on the wall. Salute and give the Pledge of Allegiance.
- As the flag is slowly hoisted by a pulley attached in the ceiling of the patrol den, all sing one verse of "God Bless America."

- Turn off all the lights, then focus as many flashlights as you have on the flag, hung on the wall. Sing one verse of "The Star-Spangled Banner."
- "Let's observe 1 minute of silence as each of us think of the Scout Law and what it means to us."
- The patrol scribe calls the the roll, and each Scout answers with one point of the Scout Law.
- The patrol leader recites the Scout Oath, but starts from "... to do my duty ..." When he has finished, all make the Scout sign and say together, "On my honor I will do my best!"
- The newest and the oldest Scouts of the patrol recite the Scout Oath together.
- The newest Scout lights three candles on a stand as all recite the Scout Oath.
- Cut out from cardboard or plywood a large Scout badge. Hang it on the wall or put it on a stand. Face it, salute, and sing "Hail, Hail, Scouting Spirit."

CHECKING. This is your "business" period. Make it short and sweet.

- The patrol scribe checks the attendance and records it. One hundred percent? Good! He then reads from the logbook his account of recent happenings in the patrol.

Everybody involved in CHECKING should move with precision and dispatch.

- The assistant patrol leader checks off all advancement tests passed by the Scouts since the last meeting.
- The patrol treasurer collects dues and reports on the patrol's finances.
- The patrol leader checks on uniforming. How many patrol members in complete uniform? All badges and insignia correctly placed?

COACHING. This is the most important part of the patrol meeting. This is where every patrol member learns something new or practices something old. This is where you work together as a whole patrol group or by buddy teams on Scoutcraft skills. This is where much of your patrol advancement takes place.

The coaching period must fit the needs of your Scouts.

During COACHING, your Scouts should learn something new and practice something old.

Occasionally, all may want to work together on mastering the same skill or earning the same skill award. But most often, each Scout may want to finish up his own tests.

From the checking of advancement that was just done in the previous period, you know what tests each patrol member has passed and what tests each needs to meet to complete his next skill award or rank. Joe and Bill, let us say, need bandage practice for the First Aid skill award. Jack, Charlie, and Pete need map and compass work for Hiking. Bob and Joe need to show how to handle the flag of the United States to earn Citizenship.

Here's their chance to finish up. To help these Scouts advance, you could:

- For Joe and Bill, have on hand a copy of *The Official Boy Scout Handbook*, two practice gauze pads, two neckerchiefs, red marker pen. Place red marks on boys' heads, hands, knees, feet to indicate wounds. Have them follow the pictures on *Handbook* page 371. Check them off for each bandage laid correctly.

- For Jack, Charlie, and Pete, have on hand three *Handbooks* and three orienteering compasses. Have them help one another to learn to use map and compass together by following the text and illustrations on *Handbook* page 193. Then have them answer the questions on page 195.

- For Bob and Joe, have on hand an American flag, halyard fastened to pulley in ceiling, one *Boy Scout Handbook*. Have them show you raising, lowering, and folding the flag (page 419), hanging the flag (page 423), carrying the flag (page 421).

You will find many more suggestions on introducing advancement into your patrol meetings in the chapter on "Patrol Advancement."

As a PROJECT, your patrol may work on a model of your favorite campsite.

PROJECTS. There's no limit to the kinds of projects an ambitious patrol can tackle.

Here are a few easy ones:

- Have each Scout whittle a neckerchief slide with the patrol animal on it.

- Make a stencil of the patrol animal. Use it for identifying your equipment.

- Whip the ends of short pieces of rope. Then tie the ropes into knots and mount them on a piece of plywood for a patrol knot board.

- Make a large patrol meeting "clock" for a wall decoration in your patrol den and to use for keeping the meeting on the right track.

- Have each Scout show his inventive genius by making a camp gadget from a tin can, a piece of wire, and a nail. Have tin snips and other tools on hand.

- Make models of all the fireplaces shown on page 113 of your *Boy Scout Handbook.*

- Make models of the bridges and other pioneering structures on page 97 of your *Handbook.*

- Make individual shields from plywood, for decorating the walls of the patrol den, showing each Scout's advancement record.

And here are some suggestions for big projects your patrol can carry out:

- Build a model of an ideal patrol camp, each Scout making one item.

- Build a patrol equipment chest.

- Make furniture for your patrol den.

- Paint and decorate your patrol den.

- Design patrol tents. Make patterns, cut materials, and sew the tents.

- Get each Scout busy making his own backpack or pack frame.

- Carve a large totem pole for your patrol's favorite campsite.

PLANS. Next comes planning for the future. Everyone should get a chance to have his say. Make your decisions by majority vote.

You may need to talk about things like this:

- The program for our next patrol meeting. Each Scout will have a leadership part.

- Our next patrol hike: What kind will it be? Where will we go? What will we take? Where and when will we meet? When will we return? The hikemaster has a number of proposals.

- Our next overnight camp: Lots of planning. Menu, food list, arrangement for purchasing. The grubmaster has suggested details worked out. Equipment: the quartermaster already has made a list. Transportation, if needed. Activities.

In making the PLANS for a hike, study your route on a topograhic map.

- How about developing and rehearsing a skit for the next troop meeting? The cheermaster has an idea.

- How can we earn money for needed patrol equipment? The treasurer gets back into the act.

- Let's get moving on a real patrol Good Turn.

- Advancement: How and when do we all become First Class Scouts? The assistant patrol leader has a chart ready to show how.

- How do we win the troop contest?

- How can we help our Scoutmaster? The patrol leader has a plan.

PLAY. Now it's time for play. "All work and no play makes Jack a dull boy." It makes a pretty dull patrol, too.

That's why you need games and singing and yells to put fun and fellowship into your patrol meetings. This is where your cheermaster will shine!

Games. You probably know a score of games and can regularly find new ones in the pages of *Boys' Life*.

There's a selection of some of the best games for patrol meetings starting at the end of this chapter. Use as many of them as you have time for.

You don't have to wait toward the end of a patrol meeting to spring a game on your Scouts. Use a game whenever you feel that a little more excitement is needed.

Pick your games to fit the situation and the mood:

- One or more Scoutcraft games in the subjects you trained in during coaching, or in the theme the troop is using for the month.

- A physical fitness game to blow off steam.

- Perhaps a "brain" game that will challenge the wits of your Scouts.

- And certainly a game just for the fun of it.

The PLAY period should be full of fun and laughter. Play games by buddies or half-patrol teams. Sing songs, practice patrol yells.

Singing. Unless your patrol knows how to sing and likes to, don't consider it a real patrol!

Use part of each patrol meeting to practice the old favorites and learn new ones so that you're ready to sing on hikes, in camp, and around the campfire.

● Encourage each Scout to get his own copy of the *Boy Scout Songbook.*

● Challenge each Scout to bring in a new song and teach it to the whole patrol.

● Develop a collection of a dozen or more songs you all like to sing. Have them rehearsed and ready whenever a song is called for at a troop activity. Learn to harmonize.

● When a suitable tune appeals to all of you, turn it into a patrol song by making up real patrol words for it.

● Make an artificial campfire for your patrol den. Gather around it for a sing-song from time to time.

Yells. Of course, your patrol should have its own yells. Practice them regularly.

You will find a number of suggestions at the end of the book.

CEREMONY for closing. And so you come to the end of the meeting. Wind it up with a ceremony. Use one you didn't use for the opening. Close the meeting in a spirit of true fellowship.

● Close with your patrol yell.

● The patrol leader says, "Be prepared!" The Scouts, in unison, answer, "We ARE prepared!"

● Form a circle with the patrol flag in the center. Each Scout grasps the flagstaff with his left hand, salutes with the right. All sing the patrol song.

Finish with a CEREMONY. The glow of an artificial campfire will add greatly to the spirit at the closing of an indoor meeting.

- Form a circle. Cross your arms in front of you. Grasp the left hand of your left neighbor with your right hand and the right hand of your right neighbor with your left. All sing the "Scout Vesper" song (in the *Boy Scout Songbook*) while swaying to the rhythm of the tune.

- Form a circle around an artificial campfire and sing "Taps" (in the *Boy Scout Handbook,* page 148). Raise your arms slowly as you sing ". . . from the lake, from the hills, from the sky." Lower them slowly as you close with ". . . safely rest. God is nigh."

What'll We Do Next? The meeting is over. It was good, wasn't it? But you want your next patrol meeting to be even better.

Feedback will help you. After each meeting, ask your Scouts what they thought of it. Did everyone participate? Was there enough variety?

If you ask each Scout how he felt, you'll get a clearer picture of what you're doing right and what can be improved.

PATROL MEETING GAMES

Most of these games are designed in such a way that the game leader can take part in them. Simply announce the name of the game, read aloud the *Action*— and go to it! Give every Scout in the patrol a chance to be a game leader from time to time.

NOTE. If you hold your patrol meetings outdoors, you can also use the games in the hiking and camping chapters and at the end of the book.

Scout Law Games

Scout Law Relay. Half-patrol teams.

Equipment. For each team, 1 pencil; 1 set of 12 slips of paper numbered from 1 to 12, placed in a pile in front of team.

Action. On signal, first Scout runs to pile, draws slip, reads number, writes on slip point of Scout Law of that number, drops paper beside pile, runs back to tag next Scout who repeats performance. And so on, until all 12 slips are answered.

Scoring. First team finished with most correct answers wins.

Newspaper Study. Half-patrol teams.

Equipment. For each team, 1 newspaper; 1 pair of scissors; 1 pencil.

Action. On signal, teams have 10 minutes to search for news items which illustrate points of the Scout Law lived up to. Items are torn out, trimmed, and numbered according to number of Law.

Scoring. Team with most clippings in given time wins.

Knot Games

Knot Loop Relay. Half-patrol teams.

Equipment. 1 2 m rope for each team.

Knot-tying relays and other rope games are always popular with Scouts.

Action. Teams in relay formation. On signal, "Square knot (or sheetbend)—Go!" Scout No. 1 ties rope into a loop using the knot called for, passes it down over his body, steps out of loop, unties knot and passes rope to Scout No. 2 who repeats the process. Continue until eight knots have been tied.

Scoring. First team with eight correct knots scores 100 points. Subtract 20 points for each incorrect knot.

Knot-Tying Relay. Half-patrol teams.

Equipment. 1 staff lashed between two chairs (or posts); 1 2 m rope per team.

Action. Teams in relay formation, 5 m from staff. On signal, "Clove hitch (or two half hitches)—Go!" Scout No. 1 runs up, rope in hand, ties rope to staff using the knot called for, unties it, runs back, gives rope to No. 2 who runs up, repeating process. Continue until eight knots have been tied.

Scoring. As for Knot Loop Relay.

Knot "Champ-Nit." Individuals.

Equipment. 1 2 m rope for each player.

Action. Leader calls the name of a knot for joining: square knot, sheetbend, surgeon's knot, fisherman's knot (*Boy Scout Handbook*, page 91). Each Scout ties the two ends of his rope together using the knot called for, drops the rope on the floor, and raises both hands.

Scoring. Winner steps out. Rest of patrol repeats the game with same knot, the winner stepping out each time, until only one Scout is left—the patrol "champ-nit." This method may be used for numerous Scout subjects. The merit of it is that the Scout most in need of practice gets most of it.

Knot Steps. Individuals.

Equipment. 1 2 m rope for each Scout.

Action: Line up Scouts at one wall of the den. Call out the name of a knot. Each Scout who ties his knot correctly takes one step forward. Leader calls another knot and the same procedure is followed.

Scoring. First Scout to reach opposite wall wins.

Bowline-Sheetbend Draw. Buddy teams.

Equipment. 1 2 m rope for each Scout.

Action. On "Go!" each Scout ties bowline around own waist. First man of each buddy team to finish joins the rope end from his bowline to his partner's with sheetbend. Both lean back with hands in the air.

Scoring. First team to finish wins.

One-Hand Knotting. Buddy teams.

Equipment. 1 2 m rope for each Scout.

Action. Buddies face each other with rope in right hand, left hand in pocket. On signal, they attempt to tie their ropes together using square knot (or sheetbend).

Scoring. First team to succeed wins.

First Aid Games

Two-Man-Carry Relay. Three-man teams.

Equipment. None.

Action. Scouts numbered 1, 2, and 3. On signal, 1 and 2 carry 3, using four-hand carry, to opposite wall and back to starting line. Next, 2 and 3 carry 1, and finally 3 and 1 carry 2.

Scoring. First team to complete three carries wins.

Triangular-Bandage Relay. Half-patrol teams.

Equipment. 1 neckerchief for each team.

Action. Teams in relay formation, each facing a seated "patient" across the room. Leader announces bandages to be tied: hand, head, knee, foot. On signal, first Scout runs up, applies first bandage, is scored by leader, unties bandage, runs back, touches off next Scout, who runs up to apply next bandage. Continue until four bandages have been applied.

Scoring. Score for quality, not speed. Perfect bandage, 10 points; good, 8; fair, 6.

Use games to teach your Scouts the two-man carry and triangular bandaging.

Arm-Sling Relay. Half-patrol teams.

Equipment. 1 neckerchief for each team.

Action. Teams in relay formation, facing a "patient" from each team across room. On signal, first Scout runs to patient and applies arm sling. When leader sees sling correctly applied, he calls, "Off!" Scout removes sling, runs back to touch off next man. Continue until four slings have been applied.

Scoring. First team finished wins.

Compass and Map Games

Compass Change. Whole patrol.

Equipment. None.

Action. Scouts form circle facing inward. Each Scout represents a main compass point (N, NE, E, SE, S, SW, W, NW), except the "it" who stands in the center. "It" calls out two compass points. The Scouts representing the points attempt to change position, while "it" tries to take the place of one of them. Scout left without place in the circle is the next "it." The other two change names to fit their new places.

Scoring. None. Repeat until all know the points.

Compass Facing. Individuals. "Champ-nit" game.

Equipment. None—but one wall of den is designated North (0° or 360°), the others East (90°), South (180°), and West (270°).

Action. Scouts stand scattered around room. Leader calls out a number of compass bearing degrees, one after the other. Scouts face the directions called.

Scoring. After each call, Scout facing bearing most correctly drops out. Last to remain is patrol "champ-nit."

Map Symbols Race. Half-patrol teams.

Equipment. For each team, 1 large sheet of paper listing the names of 20 map symbols; 1 pencil.

Compass and map games are good training for hiking and orienteering.

Action. Teams in relay formation, facing lists taped to opposite wall. On signal, Scout No. 1 runs up, draws a symbol next to its names. He runs back, touches off next Scout who runs up—and so on, until all symbols are drawn.

Scoring. Score 2 points for each correct symbol, plus 10 points for team finished first.

Map Reading. Individuals.

Equipment. For each Scout, 1 *Boy Scout Handbook;* 1 strip of paper (for measuring); 1 pencil.

Action. On signal, each Scout opens up his *Handbook* to page 195 and answers the seven questions on the page.

Scoring. First Scout to finish with most correct answers wins.

Observation and Memory Games

Kim's Game. Individuals. (Read first about Kim's Games in your *Boy Scout Handbook*, page 244.)

Equipment. 20 small items; 1 cloth to cover them; 1 pencil and 1 piece of paper for each player.

Action. Leader spreads items on a table and covers them with cloth. He lifts the cloth for 1 minute, then covers the items again. Each Scout has 2 minutes to list as many items as he can remember.

Scoring. 1 point for each item correctly listed. Highest number wins.

Nature-Picture Kim's Game. Individuals.

Equipment. 1 *Official Boy Scout Handbook*, 1 neckerchief to cover it. 1 pencil and 1 piece of paper for each Scout.

Action. Leader opens *Handbook* to page 245 (signs and marks of animals) or to any one of the *Handbook's* color pages of animal and plant life (pages 259 to 309). He covers the page with a neckerchief, then runs the game as regular Kim's Game.

Scoring. As for Kim's Game.

Kim's Game and Haunted House encourage your Scouts to observe and listen.

The Peddler. Individuals.

Equipment. 1 suitcase containing 10 to 15 articles; 1 pencil and 1 piece of paper for each player.

Action. A Scout, acting "The Peddler," enters the patrol meeting room with his suitcase. He drags out the items with a steady stream of sales talk, then throws them back in, and disappears. Scouts make a list from memory of articles, in the order in which they were shown.

Scoring. Scout with best list wins.

The Storyteller. Individuals.

Equipment. 1 pencil and 1 piece of paper for each Scout.

Action. Leader tells a story to the patrol. While telling it, he does several things, such as mopping his brow, blowing his nose, buttoning his shirt, etc. When story is finished, Scouts are asked to list things he did in the order in which he did them, rather than what he said.

Scoring. Scout with most accurate list wins.

Haunted House. Individuals.

Equipment. Blanket hung up as a curtain; various props for making sounds. 1 pencil and 1 piece of paper for each player.

Action. Players sit in front of curtain. Behind curtain, one or two Scouts make sounds with props—turn pages of newspaper, drop coins, strike match, hammer nail, break stick, etc. After 10 sounds, Scouts list those recognized and remembered.

Scoring. 3 points for each sound correctly recalled. Highest score wins.

What Do I Feel? Individuals.

Equipment. 10-15 small articles (marble, coin, Scout knife, nail, key, etc.). 1 pencil and 1 piece of paper for each player.

Action. Scouts form a circle, with hands behind their backs. Leader places one item at a time in first Scout's hands. Scout feels the item and passes it to next in circle. When all items have made full circle, leader takes them back. Each Scout then lists the items in the order he received them.

Scoring. 10 points for each correctly listed item. Highest score wins.

Wheelbarrows, Grasshoppers, and Izzy-Dizzies provide fun and excitement.

Fun and Fitness Games

Wheelbarrow Race. Half-patrol teams.

Equipment. None.

Action. Teams in relay formation at starting line, 5 m from turning line. On signal, No. 1 from each team places his hands on floor. Scout No. 2 lifts No. 1's legs at ankles. They race to turning line, No. 1 walking on his hands. At turning line, players reverse positions and race back, touching off second pair. Continue relay until four wheelbarrows have been run.

Scoring. Team first to finish wins.

Izzy-Dizzy Relay. Half-patrol teams.

Equipment. None.

Action. First Scout in each team runs to line 5 m away, puts finger on floor, circles around finger seven times, races back, touches off second Scout, and so on.

Scoring. First team completing eight laps wins.

Grasshopper Relay. Half-patrol teams.

Equipment. 1 Scout cap for each team.

Action. Team in relay formation. First Scout puts the cap between his knees and holds it firmly in place while hopping to line 5 m away and back. Here he turns cap over to next Scout who repeats action. And so on.

Scoring. First team completing eight laps wins.

Stick Fight. Two-boy game.

Equipment. 1 2 m staff.

Action. Contestants face one another, feet in a wide, firm stance. They grasp staff firmly with both hands, left hand on inside of other's right hand. On signal, each player tries to force tip of staff to ground on his right side by pushing down with right hand and pulling up with left.

Scoring. Two out of three touches wins.

Stick Pull. Two-boy game.

Equipment. 1 2 m staff.

Action. Contestants sit on ground, each bracing the soles of his shoes against opponent's. They hold staff as for Stick Fight. Object is to pull opponent into upright position.

Scoring. Two out of three pulls wins.

Belt Tug. Two-boy game.

Equipment. 2 Scout belts.

Action. Contestants, on all fours, face one another. Two belts are looped together, and the loop is placed over the heads of the contestants. The object is for each contestant to pull the loop off the opponent's head without rising from all fours or touching the belt with the hands.

Scoring. Two throws out of three pulls wins.

Special strategy is needed to become good at Indian hand-wrestling.

Dual Games

These two-boy games have these two things in common:
  Equipment: None.
  Scoring: Two throws out of three determine the winner.

Indian Hand Wrestling. *Action.* One contestant places the outside of his right foot against the outside of the other's right foot. Both brace themselves by placing their left feet a long step to the rear. They grasp right hands and attempt to throw one another. Object is to make the other move his feet or lose his balance.

One-Legged Hand Wrestling. *Action.* Each contestant holds his left leg behind him in his left hand, grasps the other's right hand with his right hand. Object is to throw the other.

Cock Fighting. *Action.* Each contestant stands on his right leg only and holds both hands on the back. Object is to upset the opponent by pushing with shoulders and upper arms only.

Indian Leg Wrestling. *Action.* Contestants lie on their backs, side-by-side, facing in opposite directions. On signal "One," they raise their touching legs to vertical position and lower them again. On "Two," they repeat this action. On "Three," they raise their touching legs quickly. Each contestant locks legs with opponent and attempts to twist him over.

Duck Fight. *Action.* Contestants squat and grasp their ankles with their hands. On signal, they try to knock one another off balance or cause opponent to release hold on his ankle.

Hand Slap. *Action.* Contestants stand facing each other, with their hands extended, one player's palms up and the other player's palms down on top of the first player's hands. The object is for the player whose hands are palms up to quickly slap the back of the other player's hand or hands before he can move them out of danger. If he succeeds, he scores a point; the hands return to original position and he tries to score another point. If he misses, the other Scout turns his palms up and becomes the aggressor.

It takes speed and quick determination to win in Indian leg wrestling.

Chapter 5

Happy Hiking

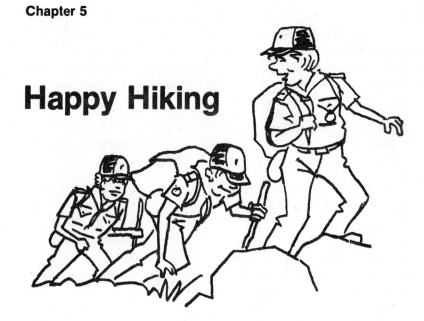

Open up your *Official Boy Scout Handbook* to the "Let's Go Hiking" section. It starts with a pertinent question, "Why hike?" and answers it immediately, "Because you are an American boy! Because there's roaming in your blood. Because hiking gives you an outlet for your roving spirit."

The boys in your patrol feel the same way. They joined Scouting to have the chance to have fun in the outdoors.

So, come on out! Out to explore, to learn the skills of Scouting, to get ready for backpacking, to take pictures, or just to enjoy the outdoors! Let's go somewhere! The real place for Scouting is outdoors!

Your enthusiasm counts. The secret to happy patrol hiking is a patrol leader who is enthusiastic about hiking, who knows how to hike, who wants to have others share in the fun he has.

If you got your early hike training in a troop with a strong outdoor program, in a patrol that did a lot of hiking under a patrol leader who knew how to lead good hikes, you're in luck. You can then use all the experience you have to make each hike of your own patrol a success.

Of even more help to you as a patrol leader will be the hikes you will have with the other members of the patrol leaders' council—the other patrol leaders, with your senior patrol leader and Scoutmaster in charge (as described in the chapter, "The Patrol and the Troop"). These leaders' hikes will contain all the features that your Scoutmaster will expect the patrol leaders to put into their hikes.

Your hike leadership. Your first actual patrol hike leadership probably will be tested on a troop hike or overnight camp. As part of the program, each patrol may be sent out on an exploring expedition, or on a *Treasure Hunt*, or on a *Lost-Child Search*. Then it's a matter of knowing exactly what's expected of you as you try to bring your patrol in the winner.

Eventually, when your Scoutmaster has satisfied himself that you have all the qualifications he expects of you, you may have the chance to take your patrol on independent patrol hikes.

Different Scoutmasters have different expectations of their patrol leaders. Some Scoutmasters feel that these are reasonable expectations:

- You must have earned your First Class rank.
- You must have experience on at least three troop hikes and one leaders' hike.
- You must have had at least 1 month's experience as patrol leader.

Before you set out with your patrol, your Scoutmaster may further insist on these points:

- You must have the written consent of the parents of each of your Scouts. (You may be able to arrange for written consents that'll do for the length of your patrol leadership.)
- You must be reasonably familiar with the countryside to be covered.
- If you plan to build fires and cook, you must have the permission of the property owner.

Planning Your Patrol Hike

Up until the day you became a patrol leader, all the patrol hikes you took part in were planned in your old patrol, under your old patrol leader. If the planning sessions you had then and the hikes that resulted turned out good, you are at a great advantage. All you have to do now is "doing what comes naturally."

So at the patrol meeting where you are to plan for an independent patrol hike, open up your *Official Boy Scout Handbook*, and spread it open to page 176. There you are: "Planning Your Hikes." Go through the suggested eight points with your Scouts:

- *What do we want to do or learn or accomplish?*
  You may want to train in some specific Scoutcraft. You may want to meet Hiking skill award requirements. You may want to study nature or go exploring. Or you may want to hike for the sake of hiking.

- *What permission do we need?*
  You have the Scoutmaster's permission. You need the permission from the parents of each Scout. Such permission may be good for the whole season. And you need a permit if you intend to light a fire.

- *What's our destination? How will we get there?*
  For your first few hikes stick to familiar places. After those, go where most of your Scouts have never been. See new things. Meet new people. Get the fun and adventure of real exploring. But some patrol members may have an idea that should be considered. If you need to get transportation to get to the start of your wilderness hike, you may find a couple of parents willing to take you there. In any case, be certain that your Scouts tell their parents where you are going.

- *What will we do on the way? And when we get there?*
  Turn to the Hiking skill award pages in the "Patrol Advancement" chapter, pages 131-32. You will find a number of suggestions there. And there are games at the end of this chapter for you to use on the hike.

- *What uniform will we wear? What other clothing?*

Your *Official Boy Scout Handbook* tells you (page 177). But just to be safe, here are some extra suggestions to take up with your Scouts:

If the weather is cold, make sure everyone has a warm jacket. Raincoats or ponchos are a must if there's a chance of rain. And in hot sun, be sure everyone wears a neckerchief to protect the back of his neck, just as the old-time American cowboys did. Head protection is important, too. You're a candidate for a headache if you don't wear a broad-brim hat, or at least a cap with a visor, when the sun glares. And you'll feel frigid if you're bareheaded on a cold day, no matter how warm your clothes are.

One more tip about clothing. Even on a cool day, you work up a sweat hiking uphill. On the hilltop, a mere breeze can cut like an Arctic wind on your wet back and chest. You'll soon be shivering. So it's smart to keep a dry shirt and at least a light jacket in your knapsack, and change when you get sweat-soaked.

- *What equipment do we need? What food do we take?*

That depends on where you're going, and how far. At least you'll want a lunch and a canteen of drinking water. Most times you'll want a map, and certainly a watch. Give advice to your Scouts who are going on their very first hike. But leave them some freedom to choose. Let them learn by bringing too much.

For the lunch, you may bring along an ordinary sandwich, an apple or an orange, and a cookie. Or you may try the trail snacks that backpackers use: sweet "gorp" mix of raisins, nuts, candy-coated chocolate. Or dry "gorp" of diced hard salami, diced hard cheese, nuts, goldfish cracker. If you plan to cook a hot meal, you will, of course, bring the necessary cook gear and food.

- *When will we take off?*
  Set the exact time for starting your hike. Insist on precision. You may be instrumental in starting your Scouts on a worthwhile habit that will be invaluable to them in their adult life.
- *When will we be back home?*
  You can't set an exact time. But you can work out an approximate time for getting home. Be sure that each of your Scouts writes down the time and tells his parents about it. Then do everything possible to have your Scouts home at that time. If they are, so that their parents won't have to worry about them, you will have gained the parents' confidence. And their willing agreement to let their sons participate in your future expeditions.

There you have it! You have planned your hike. Now hike according to your plan and make use of all the suggestions that follow.

Happy hiking to you and your patrol!

Hints for the Trail

On a patrol hike, the patrol stays together. That does not mean that you walk in a clump or in a line, one Scout stepping in the heels of the one ahead of him. It simply means that all the Scouts of the patrol are within sight of one another so that no one will ever be left behind.

The formation of the patrol depends on the circumstances.

ON THE HIGHWAY. You often may have to follow a highway for a while before you can break off onto a trail. There the rule is absolute: the patrol walks in single file, on the left shoulder, off the surface of the highway. That's the law in practically every state. The person responsible for the safety of the group walks first. That's you: the patrol leader. Since you can't look two ways at once—forward for oncoming cars and backward to be sure the last Scout is with you—that last Scout should be the next in responsibility; your assistant patrol leader.

If the patrol must cross the road for any reason, you send lookouts to any roadbends ahead or behind, and wait for their "all clear" signal before letting the patrol cross. (When the patrol does cross, everyone goes at once, shoulder to shoulder.)

ON A BEATEN TRAIL. When you get off the highway to follow an established trail through the landscape, the rule is "This is a trail. Keep it narrow." That also means single file.

Who goes first? Since the established trail is as plain as your nose on your face, any Scout can lead on.

You may, for instance, want to put your slowest hiker up front to set the pace. This is because a patrol tends to get strung out, with smaller and slower Scouts lagging behind. We all like to be first, so your faster hikers may forget about waiting for stragglers.

Or your patrol hikemaster can control the pace if you put him at the head of the line after privately explaining just what you want him to do. Tell him to look back often and make sure the rear guard is in sight.

Who goes last? That depends. But it shouldn't be your slowest hikers. One of them may have trouble with his pack. Or he may stop for a drink or to fix a blister.

Whoever is the rear guard should carry the first aid kit and extra twine to fix any pack that needs repairing.

B P

Who's in the middle? Long ago, Baden-Powell suggested that, on a hike, the patrol leader should "lead" from the middle. Here he will be in contact with all his Scouts. Here he will know exactly what is going on ahead and in the rear. Here he can have the new Scout close to him, giving him a chance to know the boy, giving the new Scout a chance to know his patrol leader.

You may want to use the Baden-Powell method whenever you have a new Scout joining the patrol.

CROSS-COUNTRY. The situation changes when you go cross-country by map and compass, in orienteering.

Who goes first? The Scout who knows how to use map and compass to lead the patrol to its planned destination. It may be you, the patrol leader, if you have earned the Hiking skill award or the Orienteering merit badge. Or it may be a buddy team trying for the requirements.

Who goes last? Nobody. Walking single file through the landscape might establish a trail that could lead to erosion. Walking in a clump might destroy patches of tender vegetation. So the rule here is: Spread out and walk in a line crosswise to the direction you are going.

RESTS ALONG THE WAY. Whenever you stop, you give the last arrivals time to rest before you move on. In a poorly run patrol the faster hikers wait until the tailenders appear, only to start hiking again, refreshed by their rest, as soon as the tired stragglers come into view. That's not the way.

A hike isn't a race. When you see something interesting, stop and enjoy it. And take a few minutes rest every half hour or so.

Whenever you start out again, be sure to count heads and make sure no one is missing. One Scout could be off in the bushes, and return to find the whole patrol vanished. It has happened.

For the best rest, have your Scouts prop up their feet on something, so the extra blood drains away.

As for blisters, they're easier to prevent than to cure. If any Scout begins to feel a sore spot on his foot, stop immediately. Have him take off his shoe and socks and cover the tender spot with moleskin or a patch of adhesive tape. Do this as soon as you suspect that someone is getting a blister. Don't wait until you're sure!

THE UPS AND DOWNS. In hilly areas you use a different walking technique from the one you apply on a flat trail.

The higher the harder. On steep hills, keep your feet flat, instead of pushing off with your toes as you do on level ground. Zigzag or step a little sideways whenever the grade gets too steep. If you get out of breath, stop for a few seconds to catch your breath and let your heart slow down.

Downhill is different. Instead of half-running with toes pointed forward, planting your feet sideways is better now. Then your feet act as brakes, so you don't get going too fast. Also, they're less likely to slip out from under you on loose pebbles. Take short steps.

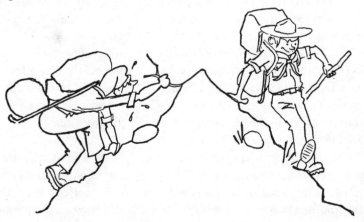

Go down switchbacks, never cut across. The straight way down is shorter, of course, but it's much more tiring because your foot and leg muscles must work hard to slow you at every step. Also, a shortcut breaks down the side of the trail, which means mudslides when the rains come.

STRANGERS ON THE ROAD. They could mean trouble. All you owe to them is courtesy—and help or information if they really need it. Be polite to everyone you meet, do a Good Turn whenever you can, but never let a stranger change your hike route, or hike with you. He may seem friendly, and still turn out to be troublesome.

NOT LOST, JUST CONFUSED. Any hiker who claims he's never been lost is either lying or hasn't been off the main trails. Even Daniel Boone admitted he got "bewildered" for a few days. But you're not really lost if you know how to find your way back to familiar ground—which isn't so hard. Read pages 210-11 in *The Official Boy Scout Handbook.*

What if your patrol goes astray and follows a goat trail that meanders off into no trail at all? Or suppose your patrol thinks it's following a route on a map, and suddenly notices that the surroundings don't agree with the map? It can happen to anyone.

It happens because you took a wrong turn somewhere. So you backtrack. Just return the way you came, and you'll probably see where you turned wrong. If not, you'll at least get back where you started. Never try a shortcut to get back on course. That could get you into worse trouble.

If you're not sure that you're backtracking, pick a landmark and have all patrol members fan out from it in different directions for, say, a hundred paces—all of you looking for something you remember passing before. One of you is almost sure to see something familiar. If this doesn't succeed, go to the nearest high point where you can get a good view.

Many Kinds of Hikes

After all your Scouts have learned how to hike properly and have tried out simple, nearby hikes, you may want to test each of the hike suggestions they have read about in their *Official Boy Scout Handbook*—an *Exploration Hike* into territory they don't know, a *Tracking Hike*, a *Beeline Hike*, a *Night Hike*. With those under your belt, here are still more that may appeal to you:

Nature hikes. Where do you live in this vast country of ours? Where the summers are hot, and the winters are cold? Where the weather is mild year-round? Where a scorching sun dries out the landscape in the summer? Where plenty of rain keeps the landscape

lusciously green? Every place will have its own kind of environment, depending on the climate. You will find all the main environments described in your *Official Boy Scout Handbook.*

Look up the environments where you live. Then make certain that all of your Scouts become familiar with them as you hike through them—their trees and flowering plants, their wildlife. If you don't know too much about the plant and animal life yourself, invite someone along who knows—maybe one of the troop leaders, a Scout parent, maybe a teacher.

The landscape features themselves also are worth knowing about. You may decide to hike toward some rock formation or mountain ridge that stands out against the sky. Get a map and look for backroads, a stream or canal, or other route off the main road. If part of a route is private property, be sure to get permission before crossing it.

Walking hikes. Sounds peculiar? Well, each of your hikes should be "Walking Hikes"—hikes on which your Scouts learn the technique of good walking. Where they build their leg muscles. Where they toughen their feet. Where they expand their lung power.

On some of your early hikes, watch how your Scouts walk. Do they lumber along like apes, with arms dangling ahead? Or do they bounce like rabbits or rubber balls, hopping straight up on their toes, pulling their feet high? Maybe theirs is the jumping-jack walk, with their knees stiff. Or the turtle walk, with head pulled in between hunched shoulders and a rounded back like a turtle's shell. Or the duck waddle, with their toes out. These styles are awkward and tiring.

Here's an easy way to change your Scouts into smooth walkers: just speed them up a little, just have them lengthen their stride a little. This will correct most of their bad walking habits. Walking faster, they naturally look ahead instead of at the ground—so, now their heads are high, as they should be. And, they naturally keep their hands out of their pockets because they swing their arms to make speed. And suddenly their chests are out and their shoulders back. They are not walking flat-chested any more, but breathing deeply instead.

They will need some practice to get rid of bad habits. But as they keep walking, their body's natural engineering gradually will take over. They'll improve automatically, almost without trying.

How your Scouts place their feet in walking is important. Duck waddle, pigeon-toed strut, tightrope walk—is their footwork one of these? To find out, have them walk on a dusty road, or in wet sand at a beach. Or barefoot, with wet feet, across a floor.

The footprints should show their toes pointing straight ahead, not outward or inward. If the prints are in one straight line as if the walker were on a tightrope, he's not walking easily, even though his toes point forward. His footprints should show his feet separated slightly, with the inner edge of each foot touching an invisible center line between them.

Lengthening his stride will help straighten out his footwork. Another trick to smooth it: look at what his hands are doing. If he walks with his hands turned out, instead of swinging naturally with the thumbs almost brushing his legs, then his toes are turned out, too. Likewise, if he carries his hands high, this means his elbows are bent too much, and his knees are pumping too much. Get him to let his hands hang loose. Swing them effortlessly.

Historical hike. Try a hike through the past. Your imagination will catch fire if you read up in advance about what happened at historical places near you. Boston and Philadelphia and many smaller cities have historical trail routes marked on city maps. In your community, the library or historical society has true stories about places where exciting things happened near you.

Mystery hike. Let 'em guess. Don't always tell the patrol where you're going. You must know, and so must your assistant patrol leader and the parents. But the rest of your Scouts can have the adventure of a mystery hike. In that case it may be a good idea for you and the assistant patrol leader (or maybe the patrol leaders' council) to try the hike on your own first. When you know all the snags, all the opportunities, all the things worth doing on that hike, it will be twice as much fun.

Flip-a-coin hike. Hikes don't always need a destination. The fun can come from the area you hike through, or activities along the way. Try a Flip-a-Coin Hike. Start down a road, and whenever you reach a fork or side road, flip a coin and go right or left. (Better keep track of your turns by sketching your route so you can find your way home.)

Foul-weather hike. Your patrol isn't a real hiking patrol if you only hike in pleasant weather. Try some hikes in storms, heat waves, freezes. Just make sure your Scouts are well prepared for the weather. Then it won't matter where you're going. Being outdoors is the adventure. Some of the happiest patrols are those that take pride in facing the worst conditions—maybe making a fire to cook lunch when all the wood is wet, and tramping home wet and tired but knowing they've toughed it out. Even if they never get the fire going, they learn something about their own manhood, and about what our pioneer ancestors lived through.

Danger!

Cars and falls. Cars are the worst hazard to hikers, of course. Can you guess what the next-worst hazard is? It's high rock formations. Too many Scouts have been killed or hurt by falls from inviting-looking crags. You, as patrol leader, must decide whether a rock or cliff is safe for your patrol. If in doubt, keep everyone off— and tell them why!

Beware of lightning. In lightning storms, remember that lightning takes the course of least resistance and tends to strike isolated objects on high ground or above the ground. Lightning is also attracted by metal, so put your equipment away from you and, if no shelter is available, sit in a low crouch with your feet close together. Keep away from cliffs and caves.

Wind-chill. On a hot, sticky day a young couple were comfortable in sneakers, shorts, and T-shirts as they climbed a mountain trail. Near the top of the mountain a cloud moved in with a rising wind. Some time later the couple was found, their bodies huddled against a stone. They died of hypothermia.

We cannot survive if our body temperature drops below 80°F. In this case, wind-chill killed this couple.

As you can see from the chart, actual chilling can begin at a normally comfortable temperature with only a moderate breeze. With a 10-mile wind and a 40° temperature exposed skin is below the freezing point of water. Surface blood vessels shut down and the skin turns white. Blood distribution lowers body temperature and if continued will bring on hypothermia. When that happens, people do strange things because blood is leaving the brain. In that condition they cannot think clearly enough to save themselves.

Your head is the most efficient radiator of heat, with your feet a close second. So, keep your head covered and your feet dry and warm if you want to avoid chilling your whole body.

Use the wind-chill chart to convince your patrol to wear or carry proper clothing for all outdoor activity.

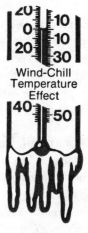

Wind-Chill Temperature Effect

Wind Speed (mph)	Thermometer Reading (°F)					
	50	40	30	20	10	0
0	50	40	30	20	10	0
5	48	38	27	16	6	—5
10	40	28	16	4	—9	—21
15	36	22	9	—5	—18	—32
20	32	18	4	—10	—25	—39
25	30	16	0	—15	—29	—44
30	28	13	—2	—18	—33	—48

Top line shows the actual thermometer reading. Lines below show the temperature that dry, bare skin is exposed to when the wind blows at the speed indicated in the left column. (For wind speeds, see page 314 of your *Official Boy Scout Handbook*.)

Dehydration. Wind-chill on a hot day is a welcome relief. Even a moderate breeze can make desert heat tolerable. Why? Our skin is one large radiator by which our body rids itself of excess heat. A breeze carries off the heat. Our sweat glands moisten the surface of the skin, and the wind evaporates the sweat, further cooling us.

More wind dries the sweat as fast as it comes to the surface. In this way we keep on losing water. It may be refreshing, but there is a limit.

Strong, steady winds can dry us out. Dehydration can make us sick. Without water and shelter from the wind we are in danger of death.

Under normal conditions we need 2 quarts of water a day. In hot windy weather we need more. So protect your patrol, carry plenty of drinking water and don't let patrol members take off their hats and shirts. Water and clothing are your best defenses against dehydration.

Heat exhaustion. Heat exhaustion hits suddenly. A fellow's face turns pale and he breaks into a cold sweat. He is sick at his stomach and his breathing is shallow or rapid.

Because heat exhaustion may be considered shock from heat, treat for shock. Place him on his back with head and shoulders low and cover him with something. Give him sips of water. Do not attempt to force water between his lips—it may choke him.

Heatstroke. Heatstroke is usually caused by long exposure to direct sun. The victim may pass out. His face is hot and dry. Breathing is slow and noisy. It may sound like snoring. He may be unconscious.

Get the Scout to lie down in a shady spot. Try to keep him as cool as possible by dousing him with water. When he regains consciousness, let him drink all the water he wants. For further care, see your *Official Boy Scout Handbook*, page 381.

It's Funny About Hardships

The hardest hikes are the ones you remember best. You'll talk about them for years afterward. Just keep this in mind if you think you're miserable.

You'll also discover that your patrol isn't as tired as it thinks. On a long hike, everyone may look like war prisoners on a death march.

But, the minute they get to their destination, instead of collapsing they'll probably roam all over, exploring caves or thickets or whatever.

Hiking Cadences

Hiking cadences. They may look tired again as they walk toward home on the last stretch of a 20 km hike. Nothing then lightens the spirit as stepping in time and sounding off: (NOTE: The words in small letters indicate the foot you put down. The words in large letters are the words you yell out.) Left LEFT, right, left LEFT, right, left LEFT, right RIGHT, left, LEFT, right. Sounding off gives Scouts a together feeling and builds patrol spirit.

The patrol can sing songs in time or try the "name sound off." You start it with the first two words, then each Scout in line shouts his name and the rest respond YO! in time. It goes like this:

Name sound off. Left SOUND, right OFF!, left JIM, right YO!, left PETE, right YO! and so it continues down the line to the assistant patrol leader who shouts: left ALL, right HERE!

Over hill, over dale. Left OVER, right HILL, left OVER, right DALE, left WE WILL, right HIT THE, left GREENWOOD, right TRAIL, left AS THE, right BOY SCOUTS, left GO, right HIKING, left A-, right LONG, LEFT! RIGHT!

Sound off! Left SOUND, right OFF, left ONE, right TWO, left SOUND, right OFF, left THREE, right FOUR! Left SOUND, right OFF, left ONE-TWO, right THREE-FOUR!

Scouting NOW hikes. New Scouts expect to get into all of the fun of Scouting right away. Smart patrol leaders take newcomers on a hike where they show them some of the skills they have learned: tracking and trailing, cooking with foil, and hiking with map and compass.

If you have an Order of the Arrow member in your patrol, he could take over this important job for you.

PATROL HIKE GAMES

Nature Games

Nature Scavenger Hunt. Half-patrol teams.

Equipment. Sealed letter for each team.

Action. Member of team opens envelope, reads letter which says: "Greetings, my friends! Your senior patrol leader is suffering from a terrible disease, acute mogigraphis. Only the magic antimogigraphia formula will save him. Bring me everything on this list within an hour from the moment you read this, or all hope is lost. (List 12 to 20 items fitting the locale and season, such as 12 pine needles, 2 bird feathers, 10 dandelion seeds, 5 dead flies, etc.) Good luck and good hunting." (Signed) Sorcerer's Apprentice.

Scoring. Team bringing in most items in 1 hour wins.

Freak Plant Hunt. Half-patrol teams.

Equipment. Pencil and paper for each team. Items for doctoring plants.

Action. In given area, "doctor" a number of different trees and plants—tying ash leaves on a tulip tree, having an orange "grow" on an oak, making daisies "bloom" on a bush, etc. (Let your imagination run wild!) Teams are then told how to find the "doctored" area, and given 10 minutes to locate these "freaks of nature."

Scoring. Team reporting greatest number of "freaks" wins.

Leaf Matching. Half-patrol teams.

Equipment. Ground cloth, laid on the ground.

Action. Teams collect one leaf only from as many different kinds of trees as they can within 5 minutes. One team places its leaves on the north half of the ground cloth, the other on the south half.

Scoring. North team Scout holds up a leaf, scores 10 points if he identifies it. South team Scout holds up leaf of same kind of tree, scores 5 points. Continue alternately until all leaves have been

Leaf Matching and Freak Plant Hunts train your Scouts to spot things that are alike or out of place.

identified and all Scouts have played. No score for a team incorrectly identifying a leaf, but other team gets 10 points for correct identification. If a team cannot match its opponent's leaf, it misses that turn. Highest team score wins.

Nature Memory Hunt. Individuals.

Equipment. On a ground cloth, spread out a nature display of about 20 items, such as: acorn cup, bird feather, small rock, dandelion leaf, large burdock leaf, bundle of pine needles, broken bird's egg, fern frond, local wild berry or nut, etc.

Action. Scouts have 5 minutes to study display, in silence, to memorize the items. They scatter for 10 minutes to collect items corresponding to display and place them alongside original.

Scoring. Scout with most items within time limit wins.

Compass Games

Silver Dollar Hunt. Individuals.

Equipment. For each participant, orienteering compass, fake "silver dollar" (50 mm [2 in.] circle cut from tin can), card with instructions: "Walk 50 paces at .... degrees (any bearing between 0° and 120°), add 120° to original bearing, walk same distance, add 120° again, walk same distance. Halt."

Action. Scatter participants over field. Place a "silver dollar" at the feet of each Scout. On signal "Go!" each Scout sets his compass for first bearing on his card and walks 50 paces. The same for second and third bearings. (When done, "silver dollar" should be at his feet, or close by.)

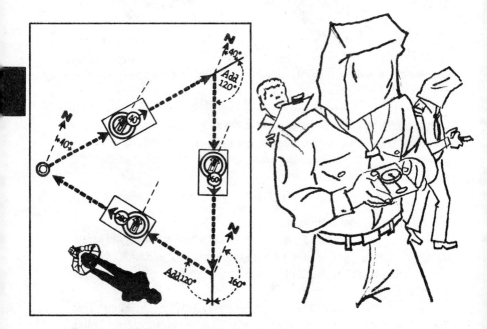

The Silver Dollar Hunt and Blindfold Compass Walk get your Scouts used to finding their way with a compass.

Scoring. Scout closest to his dollar (within 7½ paces: 5 percent error) wins.

Blindfold Compass Walk. Individuals.

Equipment. As many stakes as Scouts, placed 1 pace apart in north-south line. Orienteering compass, and a paper bag per Scout.

Action. One Scout at each stake. Half of the Scouts set their compasses at bearings between 45° and 115°, the other half between 225° and 315°. Each Scout, bag over his head and compass in hand, turns around three times, follows bearing on compass for 40 paces, then turns and follows back bearing (direction-of-travel arrow pointing toward him) for 38 paces.

Scoring. Only Scouts within 10 steps of their markers score.

Direction Finding. Individuals.

Equipment. Eight short stakes hammered into the ground on a hilltop with a wide view of the surrounding landscape, each marked with the name of a landmark easily seen from its location. For each Scout, orienteering compass, paper, and pencil.

Action. Scouts distribute themselves at the different stakes. They take the degree bearing to the landmarks indicated by the stakes and write them down. They then move to next marker and determine next degree bearing. After taking all eight bearings, they turn in their findings.

Scoring. Scout with most correct bearings (within 10°) wins.

Mini Orienteering. Individuals.

Equipment. A course through a forest with cardboard markers tied to trees giving control number, compass bearing, and number of meters to next marker. For each Scout, one orienteering compass.

Action. Scouts start at 2-minute intervals, and find their way around the course by compass.

Scoring. Shortest time wins.

Chapter 6

Camping Is Where the Fun Is

Your *Official Boy Scout Handbook* says it just right: "Camp is the high spot of your free and happy Scouting life. You'll learn more about Scouting in a few days in camp than you'll learn in months in the patrol den or the troop room."

You want the outdoor camping life that Scouting has to offer. So do your Scouts! Give it to them!

One of the greatest services you can do as a patrol leader is to turn your patrol into a camping patrol, with each Scout a trained camper. That takes time. It also takes patience and perseverance. But it can be done. And you're well on your way toward doing it the day you've made your Scouts into real hikers.

Camping is really just advanced hiking. It takes more planning and more equipment. Sleeping-out complicates matters. So does lighting fires and preparing meals. Yet the general plan is pretty much the same. As a matter of fact, every patrol hike you take is training for that greater adventure—camping. On hikes you learn to take care of yourselves—to become self-reliant. Now it's a matter of using these skills on an overnight expedition—first with the whole troop, then perhaps later with the patrol on its own. Your Scoutmaster will know when you are ready. Before starting to camp, there are two things you need to consider:

• Your patrol must have the necessary camping equipment.
• You, as patrol leader, will need the necessary training.

A few words about equipment. An experienced camper can get along with very little. He can disappear into the wilderness, build a shelter from native material, prepare his food without pots and pans, and spend the night in comfort.

It wouldn't be smart to take a group of beginners on that kind of adventure. They'll need a certain amount of equipment: personal gear, cooking pots and pans, tents.

If your patrol belongs in a well-established troop, the troop probably will have the tents that are necessary for camping. If not, you may have to hunt around for the loan of tents. Many patrols have been known to make tents of their own.

Your own camp training. There are certain standards you should live up to, certain minimum Scout experiences you should have while leading your patrol in troop camping, before your Scoutmaster will agree to let you take the patrol out camping on your own:

• You must have earned your First Class badge.
• You must have had camping experience on at least three troop overnight camps, and on one overnight camp of the leaders' patrol.
• You must have led at least five 1-day patrol hikes to the satisfaction of your Scoutmaster.
• And furthermore, before setting out on an overnight camp, you must have the written consent of the parents of each Scout.
• You must be reasonably familiar with the campsite to be used.
• You must have permission of the property owner to make camp and to build fires.

By comparing this list with the list of experiences necessary for hike leadership, you'll see that some points are the same. Others are tougher.

Your Scoutmaster will know when you and your patrol have been to troop camp often enough to start thinking about camping alone as a patrol.

Camp Planning

Planning for camp is even more important than planning for a hike. There are far more details to be covered. Again, your *Official Boy Scout Handbook* tells you how to go about it. Open it up to page 62 and settle down in your patrol meeting planning session to cover each point:

- *Personal Gear. What'll I need? How will I take it?*
  Go over the list of personal gear on your *Handbook's* page 65. Most of the items are things that your Scouts have and use in their daily life. They'll probably not all have sleeping bags, but blankets will do. Those who do not, as yet, have their own pack may be able to borrow one.

- *Patrol Gear. Tentage and cooking gear. Who'll carry what?*
  When you study the list of patrol gear on page 69, think from the beginning of your patrol organization for camp—half of the patrol as a tenting crew, the other half as the cooking crew. The

tenting crew will look after the tentage. The cooking crew will get the cooking gear together. If the troop quartermaster can provide this gear, fine. Otherwise you probably can line it up from the homes of your Scouts.

- *Menu and Food Lists. What'll we eat? What'll it cost? Who'll do the buying? Who'll do the cooking?*
  This is where your grubmaster gets into the act. You have alerted him to be ready with his recommendations. He'll have studied up on the dishes in his *Handbook*. And the two of you will have gone over the complete meal suggestions in this book (pages 170-77).

- *Transportation. Will we hike from home to camp? Or do we line up special transportation for getting there?*
  If you possibly can hike it, do so. If it is too far, get the help of your Scout parents. Check out the transportation with your Scoutmaster. An adult troop leader may be there to help you out.

- *Campsite. Where do we go? What permission do we need?*
  The hikemaster may have suggestions on this score. An owner's permission must be secured to camp on the property.

- *Firebuilding. Must we have a permit?*
  Get this permit at the same time that you get permission to use the campsite. In state and national parks fire permits are a must.

- *Time. Time of leaving. Time of return.*
  It is even more important to set these times for camping than it is for hiking (see page 88). Be certain that every Scout informs his family.

- *Permission. Parents' permission for each boy going.*
  You will need such a permission for each camp you undertake.

- *Plan of Activities. What'll we do? What kind of equipment must we take for the activities we've decided on?*
  Every camping trip you undertake is, first of all, training in camping: training your Scouts to be good campers. The way to accomplish this is to make every page of the camping section of your *Official Boy Scout Handbook*—pages 60 to 133—come alive in the lives of your Scouts.

With everything planned, with each of your Scouts knowing what he has to do, you are ready for camp.

Taking Off

You meet for the takeoff at the appointed place at the appointed time. You make a final check. "Do we have all we need—equipment, food? Are you all packed?

Getting it there. A proper pack is a "bag of bags"—or "sack of sacks." You'll find it easier to pack—and to find stuff—if your Scouts use a set of bags for grouping related items; not just clothes, but underwear, socks, dirty clothes—things like that. There's a set of plastic bags made for this use, but you can use cloth or plastic bags from the kitchen or laundry, or make 'em. Plastic is cheap, transparent, and waterproof.

When your Scouts have their gear all together, with packs to put it in, and maybe pack frames to tote them on, put them in shape to carry and to live out of. Use the personal-gear checklist, heeding the suggestions for situating stuff. (Some things a Scout—or the guy behind him—should be able to fish out at once, like a poncho, for instance.) Nothing should rattle, bang, or flop. The rig should be

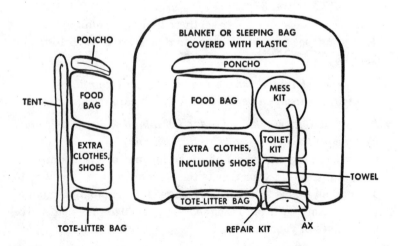

weatherproof. With forethought, the pack won't look mixed up 5 minutes after you hit camp—Scouts will be able to lay hands on just what they want. Organize! Leave room for your share of group stuff. If your Scouts don't use frames, pad the back of the pack by packing soft things next to it; they'll get to appreciate that!

Getting There

You arrive at your campsite. The ideal site has trees, water, grass-covered ground, gently sloping terrain, protection from severe weather, and a view. The possibility of finding all of these in one campsite is quite remote, but the more of them you can get in one site, the better it will be. Avoid natural hazards in picking any campsite. What's ideal in fair weather may be dangerous in a thunderstorm. Don't pitch tents directly under trees. Nearby trees afford wind protection, wood, shade, and cover for wildlife; but trees overhead will continue to drip water long after a rain, and heavy branches or whole trees can come down in a windstorm.

When you do find your campsite the natural urge is: "Let's get at it—pitch our tents and clear our fire area." Hold it, don't be too eager to get started! You don't build a house without a plan, nor should you set up camp without one. Time spent before setting up facilities can avoid later problems. A smart outfit takes a good look at the total area, using eyes and horse sense to pick the logical locations for dining fly, kitchen, latrine, and tents. Check wind direction, weather probability, and terrain. Plan your campsite for convenience and comfort.

Establish a pack line. Once you've decided where to put things, place all your packs in a neat line. This will help you keep track of

them. The first thing you'll want to do whether it's raining or not, is to set up a dining fly for the protection of packs and equipment and even for the fellows if it's really pouring. When the fly is up, packs can be opened and equipment readied for use. If a latrine must be built, a couple of fellows get started on this, a couple get wood and water, and a couple ready the cooking area. With every camper doing his share, the total job of setting up camp is simple.

Set up your woodpile where it's handy to your fire. Sort wood by size and stack it accordingly, so you can burn the right size as needed. You can peg in your woodpile to keep it from sprawling out by driving two stakes at each end.

Be sure to have a plastic sheet or light canvas tarp to throw over your woodpile during wet weather. Weight the edges with rocks or sticks of wood to hold it secure in a blow.

Menus Make a Difference

Some of the best meals you'll ever eat will be cooked and served outdoors. Good eating begins with the planning you did in your patrol den. Your menus include all the basic foods in the right amounts. They are easy to prepare over wood fire, or charcoal, by even inexperienced Scouts. They are moderately priced. They do not take too long to prepare: about 45 minutes for breakfast, 30 minutes for lunch, and not more than 75 minutes for dinner, except on special occasions.

Your breakfast is large. It's a long time between the evening meal and breakfast. It consists of fruit, cereal, a main dish, and a hot drink.

Lunch is simple—sandwiches, a salad, or other light dish. Add a simple dessert and milk or a fruit drink. In cold weather hot soup is refreshing. Usually, you want something that can be put together quickly so you can get on to other things.

Your main meal comes in the evening. You have more time to prepare it, and at this time it's more easily digested.

Let's get organized. Cooking by patrols is a lot of fun when it's properly organized. You'll find that it is a real test of the patrol

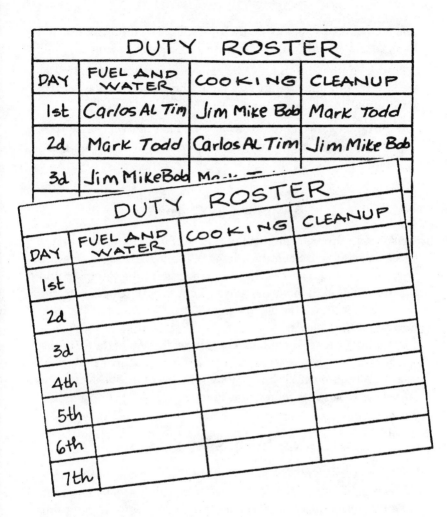

DUTY ROSTER			
DAY	FUEL AND WATER	COOKING	CLEANUP
1st	Carlos Al Tim	Jim Mike Bob	Mark Todd
2d	Mark Todd	Carlos Al Tim	Jim Mike Bob
3d	Jim Mike Bob	Ma~ ~	

DUTY ROSTER			
DAY	FUEL AND WATER	COOKING	CLEANUP
1st			
2d			
3d			
4th			
5th			
6th			
7th			

method. When each fellow has a definite job and carries it out, things go smoothly. There is a lot of fellowship and spirit stirred up when cooking and eating are involved. Even the necessary jobs of dishwashing, cleaning up, and putting things away can build teamwork and high morale when everybody does his part.

"Come and get it! When the meal is ready, your patrol sits down as a happy family. You, or one of your Scouts, say grace. Here are three you may like:

Morning. "Gracious giver of all good, Thee we thank for rest and food. Grant that all we do or say, in Thy service be this day."

Noon. "Father, for this noonday meal, we would speak the praise we feel. Health and strength we have from Thee, help us, Lord, to faithful be."

Night. "Tireless Guardian on our way, Thou has kept us well this day. While we thank Thee, we request care continued, pardon, rest."

Activites in Camp

As you go through the regular routine of a camping day, keep a check on what your Scouts are doing. Without realizing it, they are probably meeting some of the requirements for the Camping and the Cooking skill awards. Give them credit. Check off the requirements they have met on page 538 and pages 542-43 of their *Boy Scout Handbooks*.

Then fill the rest of your hours in camp with some of the activities intended for further practice in camping and cooking skills in the "Patrol Advancement" chapter (pages 133-34 of this book) and the games for camp that follow this chapter.

Rules for a Safe Camp

"Be Prepared" is the motto of the Boy Scouts of America. Preparedness is the key to success in avoiding accidents and in meeting emergencies. Make sure your camp is safe by being prepared:

- Except in rattlesnake country or in cold weather, tennis shoes are good for taking life easy around camp. Bare feet, never!
- Canned foods, soft drinks, ice chests and simliar luxuries should be discouraged as part of camping gear. A patrol which gets accustomed to them is unable to adjust for backpacking trips.
- Patrols should not have flammable fluids in camp, nor charcoal presoaked in fluid.

114

- Knives and axes should be handled carefully. Safety techniques are covered by rules to be found in Scouting literature. Sheath knives are not to be worn, and must not be used except by special permission.
- Trees, high rocks, and cliffs are climbed by adult permission only.
- Scouts leaving camp should always go in groups of three or more, with adult permission. and with a clear understanding about where they are going and when they will return. An adult should not give permission unless he knows that the patrol leader approves.
- Scouts must have clean hands when handling food.
- Dishwashing procedure is to scrape utensils clean, wash in hot soapy water, rinse in boiling water or disinfectant, set out to dry upside down.
- Cooking fires or campfires should not be left until it is so completely extinguished that the fire-tender can put his hand in the ashes.
- Scouts are expected to be in bed, and completely quiet, between Taps and Reveille. The junior staff makes a bed check, usually shortly before Taps, to be sure that no one is missing. In bad weather, this check is expanded to be sure that every Scout is dry and warm.
- No fires in tents. Even though treated, no tent material is absolutely fireproof. A tent fire can kill or disfigure. Therefore, the rule is NO FLAMES IN TENTS.

- Swimming and canoeing should be under Scoutmaster's supervision, with trained guards deployed. Horseplay should be stopped immediately and penalized.

Campfires

As patrol leader, you are concerned with both the small patrol campfire and your patrol's part in a larger troop camp or council campfire program. The patrol campfire is a great experience. The group gathers around the coals after a hard day on the trail. They swap stories and share their dreams. It's a special time.

There isn't a whole lot of planning necessary for a patrol campfire, although you may want to "keep things going" by leading a song or a cheer. A couple of the guys may want to show off a new song or stunt. It's always in order to close with a prayer to God.

While the patrol campfire is a relaxed affair, it can also be used to prepare the patrol for its part in the larger troop campfire program. You will want your patrol to be known as an all-around top patrol, and part of being a well-rounded patrol is being able to put on a top-flight skit. Your patrol, with a little imagination, can be a super

bunch of comedians, songsters, or storytellers. You're the patrol leader—show the way to campfire fun. Your patrol will be glad to follow.

Whether it is a small patrol gathering or a campfire extravaganza, all campfires follow the same basic pattern and have the same parts. A good campfire "follows the fire." It starts out strong with yells and songs as the fire roars to life, continues with skits and games as the fire is hot, and dies down to dramatic stories and quiet singing as the embers glow.

Each campfire is made up of "parts," an opening, yells, singing, skits, shorties, games, contests, and the like. Of course there are many other fun things to do around the campfire. Your patrol could be blessed with a young comedian. You might want to have a special recognition ceremony. Don't limit your imagination.

Make use of the campfire ideas in the back of this book to liven up your patrol campfires and to improve your patrol's contribution to your troop campfire. Preparing for campfires is great fun, but performing is even better. Do your best with campfires and you'll find your group can't wait 'til the next camp-out.

Rainy day campfires. What'll we do if it rains? This is a question that should be asked more often by patrol leaders. The smart patrol is prepared for rain and laughs at bad weather.

It's awful tough to have a good time around a campfire unless normal precautions have been taken for bad weather. If rain or snow threatens, collect firewood quickly and put it under a tarp. Make sure tents are up securely. Slacken the lines a bit. Put all gear in the tents or under the fly. Put your rain gear where you can get at it. Then relax. You're ready.

Patrol campfires can be held under the cooking fly. Troop campfires require more creativity. If there is a cabin or shelter around, use it. Indoor campfires lend themselves more toward inter-patrol contests, catch-on games, and skits. If it is raining and there is no man-made shelter, a short, lively troop campfire program could still be held under a large tarp. It might feature yells, singing, and story-telling. Remember, the only thing that can prevent you from having a good time is you. "Weather for ducks," properly prepared for, needn't spoil your patrol's campfire fun.

Will You Be Welcomed Back?

Good campers leave a campsite better than they found it. If you leave a piggy scene, you won't be welcomed back—and other Scouts may not be allowed to camp there either.

So, if you find trash or cans or bottles, carry them out when you leave. Burn whatever trash and garbage you can.

Unused firewood should be put in a dry place, ready for the next campers, unless you think the owner would rather have it scattered so the area looks completely natural.

Except for trampled grass and maybe the dry firewood, there shouldn't be a trace of your patrol when you leave. You bury the ashes and charred wood from your fire, after you've made sure they're cold by putting your hands in them. If you ditched tents or dug into the ground for any other reason, you carefully replace the sod.

When you're packing to go home, leave the dining fly up until last, so you'll have shelter for yourself and gear in case of rain. A wet fly is only one piece of canvas to dry.

Your own pack should contain a few plastic or cellophane bags—one for dirty clothes, another for clean stuff you haven't worn, and so on. As always, put soft things into the bottom of the pack, and heavy things on top where they'll push down the lighter stuff.

Your packing should really start before breakfast, if there's any moisture on your sleeping bag or groundcloth or rubber mattress. Check these, and put them out to dry if they need it.

If anything stays damp in a pack it may mildew and you'll never be able to use it again. So if tents are still wet when you fold them, unpack them and dry them as soon as you're home. Likewise for your sleeping bag. Any other damp stuff should go in plastic bags in your pack, and be aired at home.

Follow instructions on page 133 of *The Official Boy Scout Handbook* for a final checkout. Then line up your patrol abreast, arm's length, and make a sweep through the whole area you've used, eyes on the ground, picking up any trash you missed before.

If you do all this, one thing remains to be done—thank those who made the camp possible.

When you get home, will you look like a tramp? Or will you look as clean and sharp as if you've never been away?

Tell your patrol what old-time seamen did on the voyage home. They spent hours scrubbing the decks, polishing the brass, mending frayed ropes and ragged sails, washing themselves from scalp to toes. So when they came into port they showed no signs of having had a hard voyage. It was their way of proving that hardships couldn't get them down.

Isn't this better for your patrol than coming home dirty? You won't feel like a man if your mother moans, "Oh you poor child, you're absolutely filthy! What a terrible trip you must have had! Into the bathtub with you this instant, and then I'll help you get to bed."

Just before you leave camp, or at a stop on the way home, it's easy to wash your hands and face, comb your hair, tuck in your shirt, and straighten up your neckerchief. And it will amaze your family.

PATROL CAMP GAMES
Woods Tools Games

Split the Match. Half-patrol teams.

Equipment. For each team, hand ax, eight large wooden kitchen matches, chopping block with crack or small holes to hold the matches.

Action. Teams in relay formation 3 paces from equipment. On signal, first Scout walks up **(this is not a race)**, places a match in chopping block, picks up ax, makes three strokes with ax to split the match. After three strokes (unless he splits match with fewer strokes), he walks back and tags next Scout, who repeats the performance. Continue same way.

Scoring. Team first to split eight matches wins.

Chopper's Relay. Half-patrol teams.

Equipment. For each team, hand ax, two 15 cm (6 in.) pieces of 30 cm (12 in.) board, 2 cm (1 in.) thick, chopping block.

Action. Teams in relay formation 3 paces from equipment. On signal, first Scout runs up, picks up ax and one board, splits off strip about 6 cm (2½ in.) wide, holding board flat and using contact method. Runs back and tags second Scout who repeats performance. Continue until first board has been cut in five pieces. Continue same way with second board.

Scoring. First team to produce 10 strips with eight cuts wins.

Fuzz-Stick Relay. Half-patrol teams.

Equipment. For each team, sharp Scout knife and stick of dry, soft wood about 2 cm (1 in.) thick and 20 cm (8 in.) long.

Action. Teams line up behind knife and wood. On signal, first Scout runs to knife, cuts one sliver on the stick, lays down knife, runs back and touches off next Scout who does the same, and so on. Fuzz stick is complete when there are 20 slivers attached to the stick, each at least 7 cm (2½ in.) long.

Split the Match and Chopper's Relay are good ways to improve axmanship accuracy among your Scouts.

Scoring. First team to finish scores 10 points. Best fuzz stick scores 30 points, second best 15. To vary the scoring, deduct 5 points for each sliver cut off.

Bow Saw Relay. Half-patrol teams.

Equipment. For each team, bow saw, log about 2 m (6½ ft.) long with a 10 cm (4 in.) butt, short log for support.

Action. Teams face logs, bow saw alongside each log. On signal, first two Scouts from each team run to log. One supports the log while his partner saws off a 5 cm (2 in.) thick disk. As it hits the ground, Scouts reverse positions and saw off another disk. When second disk drops off, both race back to line and touch off next two Scouts, who repeat action. Continue race until eight disks have been sawed off the log.

Scoring. First team to finish wins.

NOTE: Use only dead, fallen wood for bow saw relay.

Fire-Making Games

String Burning Race. Half-patrol teams.

Equipment. For each team, two 60 cm (24 in.) sticks, two 1 m (40 in.) lengths of twine, two matches.

Action. In advance of race, the two sticks are pushed into the ground, 50 cm (20 in.) apart; one piece of string is tied between the sticks 30 cm (12 in.) off the ground; the other, 45 cm (18 in.) above ground. Each team gathers native tinder and firewood. Each team then selects two representatives. On signal, the two Scouts lay the fire (but not higher than lower string) and light it. After lighting, fire must not be touched, nor may more wood be added.

Scoring. That team wins whose fire first burns through the top string.

Water Boiling Contest. Half-patrol teams.

Equipment. For each team, No. 10 tin can (or other size, same for each team), 1 teaspoon soap powder or detergent, two matches.

Action. In advance of contest, each team gathers native tinder, firewood, and three rocks for fireplace. The can is filled with water to within 3 cm (1 in.) of top, with soap or detergent added. Team then selects two representatives. On signal, the two Scouts set up three-stone fireplace, lay and light the fire, place can with water over fire and keep feeding fire until water boils.

Scoring. First team to get water to boil over wins.

Fire-Striking Relay. Half-patrol teams.

Equipment. For each team, flint-and-steel set (see *The Official Boy Scout Handbook*, page 115).

Action. Teams in relay formation 5 paces from flint-and-steel set. On signal, first Scout runs up to set, strikes fire and blows it into flame, puts out fire, runs back and tags second Scout, who repeats performance. Continue until eight fires have been struck.

Scoring. First team making eight fires wins.

Fire-by-Friction Relay. Half-patrol teams.

Equipment. For each team, one fire-by-friction set (see *The Official Boy Scout Handbook*, page 114).

Action and Scoring. As for Fire-Striking Relay.

Wet-Weather Fire Building. Buddy teams.

Equipment. For each team, hand ax, available firewood, matches, pot of water, chopping block.

Action. On signal "Go!" teams drop their firewood into the pot of water, while game leader counts slowly to 10. At "10", teams pull out their drenched firewood, split it and start their fire making.

Scoring. First team to build a sustained fire wins.

The String Burning Race and Water Boiling Contest will help your Scouts to become expert fire builders.

Rope Games

Roman Chariot Race. Half-patrol teams.

Equipment. For each team, six Scout staves, nine 2 m (6½ ft.) lengths of sash cord.

Action. On signal, team lashes together a "chariot" in the form of a trestle frame, similar to trestles used in bridge building: four staves lashed into a square, fifth and sixth staves lashed diagonally to opposite sides. When frame is finished and "rein" attached, two Scouts pull "chariot" and a rider down the field around a marker and back.

Scoring. First team to finish race with chariot intact is the winner.

Tripod Suspension. Half-patrol teams.

Equipment. For each team, three Scout staves, one 3 m (10 ft.) and one 2 m (6½ ft.) lengths of sash cord.

Action. On signal, two Scouts lash the three staves into a tripod, using the 3 m cord. They then set up the tripod. Two other Scouts tie

The Roman Chariot Race and Tripod Suspension are two ways to prove that your Scouts know their knots and lashings.

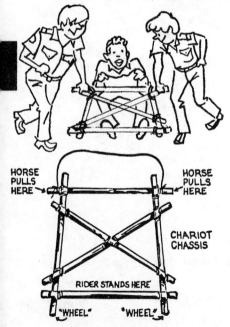

HORSE PULLS HERE

HORSE PULLS HERE

CHARIOT CHASSIS

RIDER STANDS HERE

"WHEEL"   "WHEEL"

The "Far Out" Clove Hitch is a gigantic problem in teamwork and communications for your Scouts.

the two ends of the 2 m cord into bowlines. One of them drops one bowline over the top of the tripod, the other steps into the dangling loop and keeps himself suspended by holding onto line.

Scoring. First team with a Scout suspended wins.

"Far Out" Clove Hitch. Half-patrol teams.

Equipment. A tree around which a circle with 3 m (10 ft.) radius is staked out, 15 m (50 ft.) rope.

Action. Two Scouts grasp rope at either end, which they must not let go of. They tie a clove hitch around the tree without entering the circle. Other Scouts may offer advice and raise rope as needed. This is a "fooler" requiring a lot of figuring.

Scoring. Team finishing first wins.

"Far Out" Square Knot. Two-man teams.

Equipment. For each team, one 15 m (50 ft.) rope.

Action. Two Scouts grasp either end of rope, which they must not let go of. They tie the rope ends together with a square knot.

Scoring. Team finishing first wins.

Chapter 7

Patrol Advancement

"Onward to First Class"

The moment a boy has become a Boy Scout and has joined your patrol, your task as a patrol leader is put to the test. It is up to you to make him enthusiastic about being a Scout—to inspire him, to challenge him, to see to it that his Scouting life becomes not just a happy time, but a fruitful time.

You do this by exposing him, in the patrol, to all that Scouting has to offer.

Open *The Official Boy Scout Handbook* to the section "Onward to First Class" and read carefully pages 454 to 461.

Up to now you have studied those pages from your own point of view, to help you in your own advancement. You learned that the three major groups of requirements you had to meet dealt with:

> *Scout participation*
> *Scout spirit*
> *Scout skills*

As you work with the Scouts in the patrol, you need to think of the same groups, but in a different order:

> *Scout skills* first, then
> *Scout participation* and
> *Scout spirit.*

From the minute a boy enters Scouting, he expects action! To give him this you expose him to all the *skills* of Scouting at patrol meetings, hikes, and camps. You do it so effectively that he wants to *participate* enthusiastically in all Scout activities. He stays on in Scouting. As he does so, he not only picks up the skills, but also the *spirit* of Scouting.

The skills that will make it possible for a Scout to advance to the rank of First Class Scout are the things he learns as he meets the tests of the 12 skill awards.

Those tests are not something separate from regular Scouting.

On the contrary, those tests are *real* Scouting. Particularly important are the tests involved in the five skill awards that are required for the first three ranks: Citizenship for Tenderfoot, Hiking and First Aid for Second Class, Camping and Cooking for First Class. Because of their importance, these are the skill awards you should concentrate on in your patrol activities.

But remember always that the skill awards that you and your Scouts earn are not advancement by themselves. They are *steps* toward advancement. They represent the *Scout skills* that a Scout needs to know. It is only when *Scout participation* and *Scout spirit* are added to them that they lead a Scout up through the ranks.

Scout Skills—Earning Skill Awards

Learning the skills. As you set out to help your Scouts learn the skills for earning skill awards, take your clue from pages 346 and 347 of *The Official Boy Scout Handbook*. The idea, as expressed by Baden-Powell, the founder of the Boy Scout movement, is to "give to the boy the ambition and desire to learn for himself by suggesting to him activities which attract him, and which he pursues till he, by experience, does them aright."

The *Handbook* makes all of this possible. The illustrations and the text give the Scout the chance to "learn for himself" the skills of Scouting. He gets his "learning by doing." If he runs into any difficulties, you and the other Scouts in the patrol are there to guide him. Then, after he has learned a skill in a general way, you give him a chance to improve his skill by challenging him through patrol activities that involve games, practices, and competitions. You will find scores of ideas for this on the pages that follow.

Testing and checking. As far as possible, make testing for the skills a part of your Scouts' regular patrol life.

You can have Charlie and Pete play around by themselves with map and compass for their Hiking skill award. Or you can have them lead the patrol on a cross-country hike. What's best? You can have Bill and Joe build their own little fires and cook their own little meals for their Cooking skill award. Or you can have them prepare dinner for the whole patrol. What's best? The same approach can be used for other skill awards.

As the Scout moves along, you check off the skill he has shown on the appropriate page and line in the record section of his *Handbook* (pages 538 to 548), adding the date and your initials. Also, you have it checked off on the patrol's advancement chart.

The testing and checking of your Scouts are your privileges as a patrol leader, PROVIDED *you have met the requirements yourself.* Otherwise, some other leader in the troop will have to do it. That is why it is important for you to have earned all the skill awards you expect your Scouts to take up.

Hints for the Required Skill Awards

CITIZENSHIP Skill Award: Required for Tenderfoot

Many of the requirements for this award are things the Scout has to learn for himself by studying them. They involve knowing, telling, and explaining. But a number of them are things you can make come alive in the patrol.

Since this skill award is required for the first Scout rank a boy will have to meet—that of Tenderfoot—get your Scouts interested in earning this award as soon after joining as possible. Toward this end, turn as many of the tests as you can into patrol activities, along the following lines:

- Have on hand in your patrol den a *flag of the United States of America*, large enough for correct folding.

- Without having the flag in front of them, have the boys draw a *simple sketch* of the flag from memory. Then bring out the actual flag and compare.

- Have the Scouts draw simple sketches of the *historical flags* that led up to the flag of today.

- Arrange a way of *hoisting the flag* to the ceiling of the patrol den. Then practice the correct way of hoisting and lowering the flag.

- For *displaying the flag,* impress this simple rule on your Scouts: "Consider yourself the flag. Consider your right shoulder the blue field. Always face people."

- Have all the Scouts, working in buddy teams, master the correct way of *folding the flag.*

- Have each boy, in turn, lead the patrol in the proper ceremony of *saluting the flag* and reciting the Pledge of Allegiance.

- Occasionally, use the singing of "The Star-Spangled Banner" to open a patrol meeting.

- Have the boys find out for themselves which *star* on the flag represents their own state or territory.

- Arrange for your patrol to be *flag honor guards* on occasions when your troop is to carry its U.S. flag and its own flag in a parade.

- Get permission from your school principal for your patrol to do the hoisting and lowering of the flag every day for a certain period.

FIRST AID Skill Award: Required for Second Class

Knowledge of first aid is one of the foremost things required and expected of a Scout. It is therefore important that the first aid training your Scouts get in your patrol be thorough and correct. You can't go through this subject too often with your Scouts. Repeat and repeat until every bit of first aid becomes almost second nature with them.

In testing them for the award, get the "tell" and "explain" requirements out of the way as quickly as possible. Then go into action with the "show" requirements. For these, get another Scout to act the "victim."

"Show" means exactly that. Start with the first "show" requirement, then go through the rest of them, one after the other, having the Scout repeat, if necessary, until he does each of them right.

Make further training in first aid a regular feature of your patrol program. For extra effectiveness and excitement, make up the injuries of your "victims" to look like the real thing.

- Working together in the patrol, find out the information needed to fill in the *emergency telephone numbers* listed on page 362 of *The Official Boy Scout Handbook.* Have each of your Scouts copy the list in his own *Handbook.*
- Stage an *emergency phone call* for a doctor, hospital, police, or fire department. Have each boy, in turn, pick up the phone (with the hook taped down), dial, and give the message, with you acting as phone operator or attendant. Who gives the best and clearest message?
- Bring to a patrol meeting *newspaper clippings* describing accidents. Stage the case with one of the boys as victim. Challenge the others, "What would you have done?" Have them act out the first aid they would give.

- Earn money and purchase the *official first aid kit* to add to your patrol equipment.
- Make up a *training kit,* containing a few bandages, compresses, safety pins, a pair of scissors—to be used for practice only.
- Get up a *makeup kit* to make the injuries of your "victims" look as real as possible. You'll need: Grease-stick liners—carmine to suggest abrasions and burns, palest flesh tint to show shock. Grease-paint liners—light blue for the lips of a person in shock, black for third-degree burn. Small bottle of "plastic skin"—for making blisters. Carmine tempera paint (poster color), diluted to simulate blood.
- Use the *buddy system* in your training. One boy is the victim, the other the first aider. Then change.
- Have a *first aid hike.* Send one of the Scouts ahead to stage an accident. The rest give him first aid.
- Have right-handed Scouts tie *bandages* around their right hands, then right elbows. Have left-handed boys bandage their left hands and left elbows.
- Run *first aid games.*
- Make up a *first aid dramatization* to put on at a troop meeting.
- Challenge the other patrols in the troop to a *first aid competition.*

HIKING Skill Award: Required for Second Class

If yours is an outdoor patrol that takes part enthusiastically in the troop's hikes and runs some of your own, the Hiking skill award will be a cinch for all your Scouts. After a few hikes, they'll have been exposed to all the tricks of hiking. They'll have picked up the skills of orienteering—finding their way by map and compass. And they'll have had fun.

All you need to do is to make earning the award official. You do this by checking off in their *Boy Scout Handbook's* record section what they accomplish during each hike, and finally by sitting down with them to finish up the "tell" requirements.

- During the planning session of a patrol meeting, *plan a hike* as outlined in *The Official Boy Scout Handbook*, page 176.
- Have all the boys learn the *silent signals* for formations and field work. Then use them regularly.
- Encourage your boys to wear their complete *Scout uniform for hiking. Show off your uniform proudly!*
- Take a *follow-the-rules hike.* Make it an 8 km patrol hike, sticking closely to the rules for hike speed, resting, and safety, described in your *Boy Scout Handbook* (pages 179-83).
- Secure *topographic map(s)* of your favorite hiking area.
- Mount a topographic map as a patrol den decoration. Keep on it a record of the patrol hikes you take, using red marker pen.
- Make all your hiking maps "speak *compass language*" by providing them with magnetic north-south lines as shown in your *Boy Scout Handbook* (page 192).
- For a patrol den decoration, make a *map symbols chart.* Draw the symbols greatly enlarged.
- On a patrol hike, let the Scouts, in turn, take over the *hike leadership,* following a route drawn on the map. Change leader every mile or every 15-20 minutes hiked.
- Run *map and compass games.*
- Take a *map-reading hike* to a high place with a good view of the surrounding landscape. Here, orient the map with the help of (a) surroundings, (b) compass, (c) watch and sun. Find points in the landscape that are shown by symbols on the map.
- Have all your Scouts master the three steps of using *map and compass* together *(Boy Scout Handbook,* page 193).
- Take the *cross-country hikes* described in your *Boy Scout Handbook*: Treasure Hunt (page 204), Beeline Hike and Orienteering Race (page 206).
- Write to U.S. Orienteering Federation, Box 1081, Athens, Ohio 45701, to find out if there is an orienteering group in your locality. If there is, get some of the orienteers to stage an *orienteering event* for your patrol.

CAMPING Skill Award: Required for First Class

Earning the Camping skill award is very much like earning the Hiking skill award: Your Scouts can't help earning it if they take part in the overnight camping of troop and patrol. So see to it that they get plenty of camping.

The requirements for the Camping skill award are all action. Just let the Scouts go about their camping and check off the requirements as they are being met.

- During the planning session of a patrol meeting, *plan an overnight camp,* as outlined in *The Official Boy Scout Handbook,* page 62.
- Discuss the *personal camp gear* needed for an overnight. Then have each Scout write down a list for himself.
- Have a *packing race* in the patrol. Each boy brings a fully packed pack containing all the personal gear for an overnight camp. On signal, he unpacks it, then repacks. Best pack determines the winner.
- Run a *tent-pitching contest* by buddies. Then have the winning buddies each pitch a tent single-handedly.
- On your patrol hikes, set out to find a few *campsites* suitable for patrol camping. Get permission to camp there. Strictly follow any rules the owners may set for their use.
- Get together all the *patrol camping gear* you need for successful overnight camping.
- Make a *patrol box* that can be used for storage in the patrol den and as kitchen box and worktable in summer camp.
- Organize and train your patrol for efficient camping so that it will be prepared to match itself against other patrols at a troop, district, or council *camporee.*
- Get the whole patrol signed up for *summer camp* as soon as the first registrations are due.

- Have *ropes for knot-tying* on hand in the patrol den: eight pieces of ¼-in. rope or clothesline, 2 m (6½ ft.) long for practice and for games; thin twine for whippings (electrician's twine is especially good), cord or binder twine for lashing practice.
- Have each Scout whip the two ends of his *practice rope.*
- Have *quiz competitions* on uses of different knots: "What knot would you use if ... ?"
- Announce a knot. Give your Scouts a chance to practice it, using their *Official Boy Scout Handbook.* Then run *knot games.*
- Have patrol *knot-tying competitions* for speed to see who is the fastest in the following: (a) tie a single knot, (b) tie all knots required for Camping skill award, (c) tie knots with eyes closed, (d) tie knots behind back, (e) tie most knots in 1 minute.
- Whip the ends of short pieces of rope. Tie the rope pieces into all the knots on your *Boy Scout Handbook's* page 91. Mount the knots onto a *knot board* for your patrol den.
- Make simple *camp gadgets,* using cord or twine. Start with those shown in the *Boy Scout Handbook* (page 97). Then invent some of your own.
- Eventually graduate to large-scale *pioneering,* using ¼-in. lashing ropes: *Fieldbook,* pages 104-11.

COOKING Skill Award: Required for First Class

The Cooking skill award is not just a matter of slapping a hamburger patty into a pan and frying it. It covers the whole process of preparing a meal—from planning the dishes, making the food list, preparing tinder, kindling and fuel with knife and ax, making a fire, to the actual cooking. And all of it—with the exception of getting the foodstuffs together—in the outdoors.

So the more camping, the more cooking, and the more good eating for your Scouts.

Give the Scout a chance, beginning with his very first camping trip with the patrol, to be involved in planning and preparing the patrol meals. This is the natural way for him to pick up the skills. Then, each time he meets a requirement to your satisfaction, check it off in the records section of his copy of *The Official Boy Scout Handbook* (pages 542-43).

For the most important requirement, No. 5.a. "prepare... a complete breakfast... and a complete dinner or supper... for yourself and two others"—arrange for him to be part of a three-boy team. Even better, challenge him to cook for the whole patrol.

- During the planning session of a patrol meeting, plan *meals for an overnight camp,* using the menus on pages 172-77.
- As part of your *patrol equipment*, secure two Scout axes, a file, and a sharpening stone.
- "Get out your knives. Here's a thumb-thick stick for each of you. Who whittles the best *fuzz stick?"*
- When working with fires, see to it that all your Scouts adhere strictly to the *safety precautions* for building and extinguishing a fire, as described in *The Official Boy Scout Handbook*, pages 107 and 116.
- Try each of the *fire lays* in the *Boy Scout Handbook* (pages 110-11). Which one suits your patrol best?
- Determine which of the *fireplaces* on page 113 of your *Boy Scout Handbook* is most suitable where your patrol goes camping.
- Learn by experimenting which are the best *tinder materials* in your area, and which are the *best woods* for kindling and fuel.
- Go in for *all-weather fire making.* Have a contest on a rainy day or use wood soaked in a pail of water.
- Divide the patrol into *buddy cooking teams.* Assign separate teams to each of the three meals during an overnight. Or have one team prepare all the meals.
- Try out all your *Boy Scout Handbook's* recipes for *aluminum foil and fun food cookery* (pages 126-29). Invent some of your own.
- Develop a *patrol cookbook.* Let the Scouts contribute their

favorite recipes. Give the dishes fancy names peculiar to your patrol—such as "Barking Fox Mulligan."

- Invite the parents to visit your patrol camp for an outdoor *family meal*. Treat them to the Brownsea Double-Two Feast (*Boy Scout Handbook*, page 129).

Hints for Nonrequired Skill Awards

CONSERVATION Skill Award

Although not required for advancement in rank, this is one of the most important skill awards.

Everybody's talking about conserving energy, soil, water, wildlife, and open spaces. Everybody's worried about water, air, and noise pollution.

Don't just talk or worry about conservation. Do something about it! Get your Scouts interested in earning the Conservation skill award.

Most of the requirements involve study and individual activities that your Scouts will undertake by themselves. All of these are covered in the "Protect Your World" chapter of *The Official Boy Scout Handbook*.

But when it comes to conservation projects that your Scouts will need to take part in, there's where your patrol can shine. For example:

- Put on a dramatization of the four points of the Outdoor Code. Or put up posters in parks or public areas urging good outdoor manners.
- Select a stretch of roadside, stream, lake shore, or beach where you live. Collect all the rubbish on it. Then get rid of it properly. A stretch of 150 m (or 500 ft.) is a reasonable day's goal for a patrol.

- In the inner city, adopt an *empty lot*. Find out who owns it. Get permission from the owner or city department to clean it up. Plan the most effective way, then do it.

- Protect a *low stream bank* from erosion by planting willow cuttings. If planted in spring or early summer the cuttings soon will sprout roots to hold the soil.

- Protect a *steep stream bank* by riprapping. Place a row of stones against the foot of the bank. Build a wall against the bank to the height the water might reach.

- Stop the formation of a *small gulley* by diverting the water that may flow into it. Then plant grasses, vines, shrubs.

- Repair an *eroding downhill trail* in camp by installing water bars to direct the water off the trail. Cut a shallow channel across the trail, at an angle to the slope. Then place a log or a row of stones in the channel.

- Plant *tree seedlings* on your campsite for the improvement of the area, or for future timber. Get seedlings from your state forester or the soil conservation service. Plant by buddies: one Scout makes the hole, second Scout plants the seedling.

- Under the guidance of a ranger, mark the *undesirable trees* in your council camp for cutting, and brush areas to be cleared for future campsites. Then get in there with axes and saws and follow his directions.

- Plant *shrubs* that will give food and protection to birds and animals.

- Make *brush piles* to provide cover for wildlife.

- Cooperate with local fish and game department to build *deflectors* for improving streams for game fish.

- Find out where your local *recycling center* is. Collect and bring in newspaper, aluminum cans, steel cans, and glass.

- For a *newspaper drive,* bring along pieces of cord or twine 2.5 m (8 ft.) long. Stack the papers 20 to 25 cm (8 to 10 in.) high. Tie up the bundles using the packer's knot.

 **ENVIRONMENT Skill Award**

From the very first patrol hike you undertake, get your Scouts excited about nature around them, about the environment you pass through. Some boys take a ready interest in all living things from the start. Others need to be awakened. You as patrol leader can do much to open the eyes of your boys to the wonders of nature, and maybe start them on a hobby that will last throughout their lives.

Here you have a great help in the activities suggested in your *Official Boy Scout Handbook*, and in its magnificent color illustrations of all aspects of nature.

- On a patrol hike, use a simple *nature game*, such as Far and Near, or Nature Hunt (*Official Boy Scout Handbook*, page 243) to make your Scouts become observant.

- Get your boys into the habit of *checking animal and plant life* they see against the illustrations on the color pages in the *Handbook*. Whenever they identify a mammal, bird, reptile, amphibian, fish, insect, tree, or flower have them underline the name and write the date next to the underlining.

- Run *nature games*.

- Make a "whifflepoof" (*Boy Scout Handbook*, page 249). Take up *trailing* and play the game of Hunting the Whifflepoof (page 256).

- Have your Scouts keep their eyes open for *animal tracks*. When found, try to imagine what the animal was doing when making the track.

- Make a set of *track plaster casts (Boy Scout Handbook*, page 246) for the nature museum in your patrol den.

- During your lunch break on a hike, go in for *stalking*. Play the games of Sleeping Pirate, Deer Stalking, or Wary Wolf (*Boy Scout Handbook*, page 257).

COMMUNICATIONS Skill Award

What is needed for this award is for the Scout to pass what might be called a series of "man-to-man" requirements. If you, the Scout's patrol leader, have earned this skill award it's just a matter—with the exception of No. 2: "Teach a Scout skill to two (2) or more Scouts."—of getting together with the Scout and taking him through the requirements, one after the other.

When you come to No. 3: "Get a message to others without speaking or writing using two of these..." you are all set if you know the two methods the Scout has chosen. If you don't, get another Scout who knows them and have the two communicate with each other, with you checking the success of their communication.

PHYSICAL FITNESS Skill Award

This is a completely personal award. It requires the Scout to find out and do things for himself, and to have himself checked by doctor and dentist.

Your main task is to watch and check the Scout performing the five physical fitness activities in requirement No. 2.a. and to recheck them 30 days later for requirement 2.c.

But to get him to improve his fitness is a different matter. Every patrol hike he takes part in, every patrol camp he attends, every vigorous game you plan for him to join will help him strengthen his body.

 **SWIMMING Skill Award**

Teaching a Scout to swim is normally outside the field of a patrol leader—unless you happen to be a certified swimming instructor. The best you can do is to see to it that he has the opportunity to learn.

Your best bet is to get the Scout to summer camp. Here, at the waterfront, he will get all the help he needs from qualified lifeguards. For the rest of the year, you are lucky if your community has a swimming pool. Get the Scout signed up for a course in swimming.

If the boy, when he enters the patrol, already knows how to swim, you have no problem. If you are a swimmer yourself, you can check him off against the requirements at the camp waterfront or the swimming pool, under the watchful eye of a lifeguard.

From that moment on, help him increase his swimming ability by having him, with the rest of the patrol, take part in all the activities described and shown on the "Swimming Fun" pages of *The Official Boy Scout Handbook* (pages 158-59).

 **FAMILY LIVING Skill Award**

If you have come to know the family of the Scout who wants to earn this award, you'll have no problem: members of the family will do half of the work for you. You simply ask one of the adults to date and initial each of the requirements the Scout has met at home: lining up jobs to do, inspecting his home, looking after younger children, taking part in family fun activity, helping save energy, listing emergency phone numbers.

For the rest of the requirements, simply have a friendly chat about his family, checking off the points that have some bearing on the remaining requirements.

 **COMMUNITY LIVING Skill Award**

This is an award where the requirements mostly deal with "knowing." The Scout prepares himself, then sits down with you to explain and tell you about the things he has learned.

As for the requirements that involve a visit to an organization, a public service, or the police department, you perhaps can help him set up his appointment—and possibly go with him when he pays his visit.

Scout Participation—Scout Spirit

When a Scout has earned the number of skill awards he needs for the rank he is seeking, you match his *Scout skills* with the other two major parts for advancement in rank: *Scout participation* and *Scout spirit.*

Scout participation. Each time a Scout moves up from one basic rank to another, he must be active in troop and patrol for "at least 2 months."

This "active" participation, as *The Official Boy Scout Handbook* tells you, depends on three *A's*: *A*ttendance, *A*ppearance, and *A*ttitude.

His *attendance* should have been recorded in your *Patrol Record Book* or on your patrol attendance chart. Give him a full score for the activities he attends. Give him a full score also for the activities he is prevented from attending because of sickness or some other valid reason, PROVIDED *he has informed you of his absence BEFORE the activity.* This will give you a chance always to be able to announce correctly, when patrol attendance is called for, "All present or accounted for."

His *appearance* depends a lot on the spirit you have built up in your patrol. If you expect your Scouts in uniform at all Scout activities, they will strive to show up in uniform. But then they, in turn, will expect you to be in uniform. Your example counts immensely.

His *attitude*—Here's a hint for you: "In Scouting there is no such thing as a discipline problem—but there is such a thing as a bored Scout." No Scout is bored in a patrol or troop where the program is exciting and the spirit high.

Scout spirit. When it comes to determining the Scout's spirit, ask yourself a number of questions:

How does he "obey the Scout Law..." Go over every single point. Not just the way he acts when he takes part in patrol and troop activities, but as a boy in his family, in his community. How does he live up to the Scout Oath?

Has he caught the spirit of Scouting? Is he enthusiastic about being a Scout?

Is he an asset to the patrol? Does he volunteer? Does he do what needs to be done, with a smile?

And there are many other questions you can think of by yourself.

The Final Steps

The personal growth agreement conference. When you are completely satisfied that the Scout has met all the requirements for a rank, inform your Scoutmaster.

The Scoutmaster will meet with the Scout for the same kind of friendly chat that he had with you when you moved from one rank to the next. It will follow pretty well the pattern described in *The Official Boy Scout Handbook*, pages 459-60.

The board of review. Next, the Scout appears before the patrol leaders' council, before the patrol leaders of the troop—including yourself—the senior patrol leader, and the Scoutmaster.

It's a friendly review—of what he has learned, of the way he learned it, how he likes being a Scout. And, in a way, it is a test as well of your leadership and the spirit of the patrol. The way a Scout acts at the board of review will show what kind of patrol he belongs to.

He passes with flying colors, of course! You knew he would.

At the next troop event, he receives the badge that denotes his rank.

And he and you and the whole patrol celebrate!

Chapter 8

Exit Smiling!

The time will come when you must take off your patrol leader badge. You'll be happy in a way, just as when you take a heavy pack off your shoulders. Part of your happiness is knowing that you carried the load to the trail's end. You did your job to the best of your ability.

You'll also be sad in a way. This may be the first time in your life that you've had to step out of a position you were proud to fill. And Scouts in your patrol will be sad at your going. You'll never again be quite as close to most of them.

When You Felt Like Quitting

Scientists say almost everyone gets a what's-the-use mood sometimes, as regularly as the tide and the calendar. If you were feeling down when your patrol did poorly, you thought of quitting. But nobody ever said your job would be easy. So you hung in there, and now you're glad you did. You wouldn't want to be known as a quitter.

A man named Hal Stebbins once gave good advice for leaders at all ages: "You are remembered for the hand and heart you held out to those on the way up. When you get to the pearly gates, St. Peter isn't going to ask, 'Were you in the top 10?' He is more likely to ask, 'What did you do to help the bottom 10?'"

If you've helped your patrol, the headaches and heartaches were worthwhile. Look back down the steep trail you've climbed. Look at the load you've carried. Remember the high spots instead of the low. Every time you wanted to quit but stuck it out instead, you won a battle with yourself.

So now you're a winner in ways you won't realize until years from now. You've done a lot of growing. You've learned to get along better with other people. You've sharpened up leadership skills you can use all your life.

Also, you've joined a long invisible line of boys and adults who make their community a better place to live in. You're on the same trail with the den leader and the Scoutmaster and the club president who give many hours to planning a program and carrying it out. You're like the teacher who works hard to help pupils learn; the Red Cross volunteers who go far out of their way to help people in trouble; doctors and missionaries and countless others who do a hard job because they know it may not get done if they don't do it. They feel—and so do you—that nothing is too much for the sake of service.

Sometimes You're a Hero

Remember the time you lent your jacket to a skinny Scout in your patrol because he looked cold? Remember the time a storm came up in the night, and you got out of your warm sleeping bag and your snug tent to make sure your patrol's tents weren't blown down or flooded? Probably there were countless times you stepped in to show a younger Scout how to chop wood or start a fire or pitch a tent. Your patrol members notice such things. Younger Scouts are at the hero-worshiping age, and if you're a reasonably good patrol leader they idolize you. Also they imitate you, which is good for them.

The Dividends Keep Coming

Those Scouts won't forget you. As they grow older, some may become your lifelong friends. Others may meet you unexpectedly somewhere and say something like, "I still remember things you taught me." If you need help, old friends may rally around you.

Furthermore, people will turn to you when they need someone they can trust. After working to build a strong patrol, you'll find yourself working for the kind of world that mankind is dreaming about.

What's Next?

As you finish being a patrol leader, other jobs in Scouting are waiting for you. Probably your troop needs you as a staff officer. And an Explorer post probably wants you, too. In high school and college, you'll find many organizations you can serve. Wider fields will keep opening.

So don't feel bad about leaving your patrol. Look back proudly, then throw yourself eagerly into new tasks ahead. As the Spanish say, "Go with God."

Great patrol leaders can do anything!

Part 2

TOOLS for YOUR JOB

PATROL

Games and Activities

Sample Menus

Campfire Ideas

Projects

● ODD BALL
◉ EVEN BALL

Games and Activities

Boy Scouts all over the country and around the world play these games. All of them are fun. Learn the rules of a few games and try them out with your patrol. Most of the games involve individual Scout contestants; others are played with buddy or half-patrol teams.

All of the games can be converted to patrol contests at troop meetings. At the patrol leaders' council meeting you can suggest that your patrol is getting pretty good at such-and-such game and are willing to challenge other patrols. In that way you can help build the troop program and have a good time doing it.

Fitness

Jump the Shot

Equipment. Long rope with soft weight (sandbag) in end.
Patrol circle formation, with one boy in center who swings rope around circle below knees of others, who must jump it. If hit by rope or bag, they are given 1 penalty point. At end of game, Scout with least points wins.

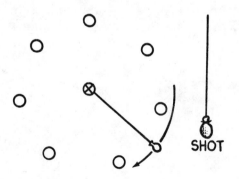

SHOT

Stiff

Equipment. Two blocks of wood.

Scouts move at will within a specified area. The leader stands where he can observe all action. When he claps the two blocks of wood together loudly, all Scouts freeze. If any Scout moves, the leader shouts his name. Guilty party must salute each player. Leader again strikes the blocks together requiring all action to cease as Scouts again freeze. The leader again looks for movement and shouts out the name of another Scout, if he detects motion. If he is unable to distinguish motion, he says "Mill around" which permits Scouts to move at random around the meeting place until he again strikes the blocks together.

Dodge Ball

Equipment. Large ball such as basketball or volleyball.

Scouts in circle with "it" in center. One ball is tossed to a member of the circle. Object of game is to hit the center player below the waist with the ball. When hit, he changes places with the Scout who hit him, and the game continues. When played indoors, restrict all throwing to two-handed passes to cut force of the throw.

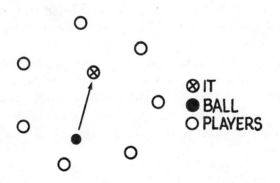

Circle Out

Equipment. Volleyball or basketball.

Scouts stand in circle with hands on knees, feet about 60 cm (2 ft.) apart, outside of each foot touching neighbors' feet. In the center of the circle is the Scout who is "it." The object of the game is for "it" to roll the ball between the legs of the Scouts and out of the circle. Scouts in circle may not move their feet or hands, but may block the ball with their knees by twisting and turning. The Scout who lets the ball go between his legs becomes "it," and the former "it" takes his place in the circle.

Ringleader

Equipment. None.

Patrol seated in circle. "It" leaves the room. While he is out, Scouts select a ringleader. Scouts make some motions as ringleader while "it" tries to determine which Scout is the leader. Leader must change motions at least every 15 seconds. Ringleader may clap hands, rub head, leg, arm, stomach, pat knee, etc. If "it" can identify the ringleader in three guesses, he can stay "it" for next round. If he fails, ringleader becomes "it."

Swat 'Em

Equipment. A wrapped newspaper or cloth sausage.

Each Scout holds his hands cup-shape behind him. "It" carries wrapped newspaper or cloth sausage to use as swatter. He leaves it in the hands of one of the players in the circle, who from that moment on may swat the boy at his right on the back, below the neck, as long as that boy runs around the circle and back to his own place in the circle again. When this chase is completed, the new holder of the swatter circles mysteriously about the ring, leaving the swatter in the hands of another boy, and takes a place in the circle.

Do-This—Do-That

Equipment. None.

Leader in front of his troop, performs certain movements, preceding each with "Do this!" or "Do that!" All movements following the order "Do this!" must immediately be executed by all players, while movements following "Do that!" must be ignored. Players making

150

mistakes step back 1 step. Continue for a certain length of time. Winner is Scout nearest the starting line.

Crows and Cranes

Equipment. None.

Divide the boys into two teams lined up facing each other, one side called the "Cranes," the other the "Crows." When the leader calls out "Cranes!" or "Crows!" all on the team named must turn and run to the wall back of them. If a boy is tagged by an opponent before reaching the wall, he is captured and becomes a member of the other team. This can be kept up until one team has captured all those on the other side. The leader can add fun by dragging out the words and by giving occasional false alarms—for example: "Cr-r-r-rows" or "Cr-r-r-ranes," or "Cr-r-rash!"

Number Call

Equipment. One blindfold.

Scouts sitting in circle formation with one blindfolded Scout in the center. Number all Scouts in the circle from 1 through the number playing, including the blindfolded Scout. The blindfolded Scout shouts out two numbers. Scouts with these numbers must change places with one another without being tagged by the blindfolded Scout. If he tags one, they change places. If not, he calls out two more numbers.

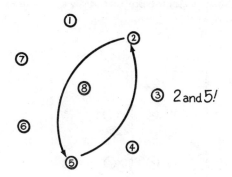

Steal the Bacon

Equipment. One neckerchief.

Two teams line up with 6 paces between the lines. Teams face each other and number through, thus there are two Scouts for each number—one in each line. Two "1's," two "4's," etc. The "bacon"—neckerchief lies on the ground in the center. The leader calls "3's," and the two "3's" dash out, each trying to seize the "bacon" and get home before the other "3" tags him. Score one point for getting home safely or for tagging Scout trying to carry "bacon" home.

Ball Over

Equipment. Basketball or volleyball.

A line is drawn across center of room or cleared outdoor area, one team on either side of the line. Players cannot cross over the line. Leader with a whistle is blindfolded or stands with his back to the action. When the whistle is blown, the Scouts toss the ball back and forth across the line. Whichever team has the ball when the whistle sounds again is penalized by scoring one point for the other team. The object, of course, is to get the ball as rapidly as possible into the other team's territory each time it comes over.

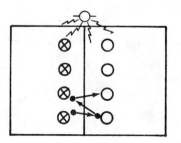

Overtake

Equipment. Two basketballs or volleyballs.

Scouts in circle formation. Number the Scouts from one to the total playing. Must have even number in the group. All even-numbered Scouts in the circle make up one team and all odd-numbered Scouts the other team. Hand a basketball to Scout No. 1. Give the other ball to the even-numbered Scout on the exact opposite side of the circle. On signal, Scouts pass balls clockwise to members of their team (every other Scout). Both balls will be traveling in the same direction. Object of the game is for one team to pass their ball faster than the other team, and eventually overtake the other team's ball.

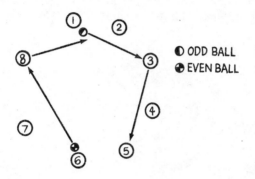

◗ ODD BALL
● EVEN BALL

Antelope Race

Equipment. None.

On signal, Scouts run in single file with one hand on the belt of the Scout ahead to a point 30 paces away, make left turn, and run back to starting point. Falling down or breaking apart eliminates the team.

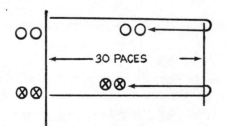

Three-Legged Soccer

Equipment. A neckerchief for each Scout, four chairs, and a soccer or volleyball.

At each end of the meeting place or field, place two chairs or goal markers about 1 pace apart. Organize Scouts into two teams. Scouts in each team pair up, their inside legs tied together at the ankle and knee with neckerchiefs. One pair on each team acts as goal tenders. Place the ball in the center of the playing area with both teams taking positions in front of their goals. On signal, each team tries to kick the ball through the goal of its opponent. The ball shall not be touched with hands or arms. After a team has scored, place the ball in the center and begin the game again. The team with the most points after a predetermined time limit is the winner.

● SOCCER BALL
■ CHAIRS

Under and Over Relay

Equipment. Ball.

Front player has a ball—or other large object—which he passes over his head, using both hands, to the player behind him, and so on down the line. When the last player gets the ball, he runs to the front and passes it between his legs back down the line. Next time, over the head, and so on. Ball must be passed, not thrown. First team to regain its original order wins. Variation: Front player always passes over and the next under, and so on alternately.

154

One-Pitch Softball

Equipment. Bats, softball, and softball diamond.

Two teams are needed with at least five players on a team, so challenge another patrol to play this game.

1. Unlike regular softball, the pitcher, who is on the side of the batting team, serves up easy pitches to his teammates. One pitch to each batter which is either a "hit" or an "out"—no strikes, no balls, no fouls. A wild pitch is an out, runners may not advance.
2. With a hit the pitcher makes no attempt to field the ball.
3. The team at bat has three outs in an inning.
4. When the third out is made, each team member taking the field must touch third base. The team coming to bat, which includes the pitcher, must touch first base.
5. If the pitcher and batter can get started before the fielding team gets into position, they may score an easy run. Quickness pays off; there is nothing slow about this baseball game!
6. The entire game is played in five innings.

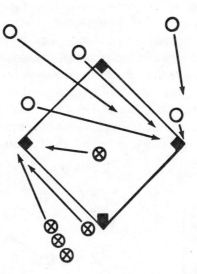

Ball Relay

Equipment. A ball or beanbag for each team.

Teams in relay formation with the team leader stationed 4 paces in front of his team line. The front Scout in each team has a ball or beanbag. On signal, he throws the ball to the team leader and ducks down. The team leader throws the ball back to the next standing Scout, and so on until all Scouts have thrown and ducked. A missed ball must be recovered by the Scout missing it. He must get back in line before throwing it again. First team through wins.

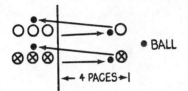

Rubber Ball Relay

Equipment. Small rubber ball and pop bottle for each team.

Teams line up in relay formation. First Scout in each team has a rubber ball in his hand. About 5 paces in front of each team is a bottle on a chair. On signal, first two Scouts in each team place the ball between their foreheads, carry it in this manner, without using hands, and deposit it on top of the bottle. Once the ball is on the bottle, one Scout picks the ball up with his hand and runs back to starting line, giving it to the next two Scouts in line who repeat the process. If the ball is dropped, the pair must pick it up and return to the starting line to start over. First team finished is the winner.

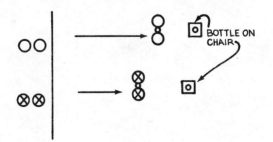

Ships in the Fog

Equipment. Chairs for obstacles, neckerchiefs for blindfolds.

Teams line up in relay fashion with first boy in each line blindfolded. Between the starting line and the far wall are numerous chairs scattered at random. On signal, the first Scout in each team tries to go through the room to the far wall. If he touches a chair, he must go around it three times before proceeding. Once he reaches the wall, he may remove his blindfold and run back to next Scout in line who is already blindfolded waiting to go. Scouts who are not blindfolded may direct the Scout who is on the "ocean" by shouting directions at him from behind the starting line. First team to guide all its members across the room and back wins.

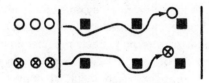

Compass

Starburst Compass Course

Equipment. Compasses, marked paper bags to be used as markers, wrapped candy as many kinds as teams, team course instructions.

Starburst 3 lets you set up a compass course with a minimum of preparation. Everything starts at station 0 and spreads outward. Each team carries the marker for its station. When it arrives at its destination it leaves the marker and continues on its course to find the markers of the other teams.

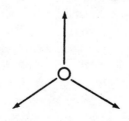

In Starburst 3, for example, three buddy teams compete. Each team carries a lunch bag with six pieces of wrapped candy and a stone heavy enough to keep the bag in place if the wind blows.

At the signal to get ready, each team stands at the starting point or station 0. Team No. 1 sets its compass to 360°; team 2 to 120°; and team 3 to 240°. At the signal to get set, each team faces the direction for its first course. At the signal go, they race off counting their paces as they go. At 85 paces each team leaves its paper bag marker with the number of the team on the bag. Each member takes a piece of wrapped candy as proof of being at that station. He may eat the candy, but must keep the wrapper. Each team, of course, should have different candy.

Then team No. 1 heads for station 2, while team No. 2 heads for 3, and team No. 3 heads for station 1. If each team follows its compass reading correctly and counts its paces carefully, it will find the marked bags. Each contestant takes a piece of candy from the marked bag to prove he found it.

The next course leads each team to the last marker. When reached, the team brings the marker back to the starting point, station 0. First team back, with the right candy wrappers to prove it, wins.

Wrapped candy is just one thing that could be used as proof of finding the marker. Slips of paper with a secret mark or signature made by the team who set the marker can be used instead.

Starburst 3 can be held in an open field, a park or wooded area. Station 0, the starting and finishing point, should be at least 140 m away from a lake, river, building, or road.

Your compass helps you to measure direction. Your double steps or paces help you to measure distance. In starburst 3 you need to measure both. Of course, not everyone's paces are the same as yours. Get your patrol members to count 85 paces with you. You may come out close to one another. If you don't, you can make accurate estimates of distance by using the distance computer on pages 574-76 of *The Official Boy Scout Handbook.*

The key to a successful starburst 3 contest is pacing off 85 paces of equal value in each direction.

Starburst 3 Instructions

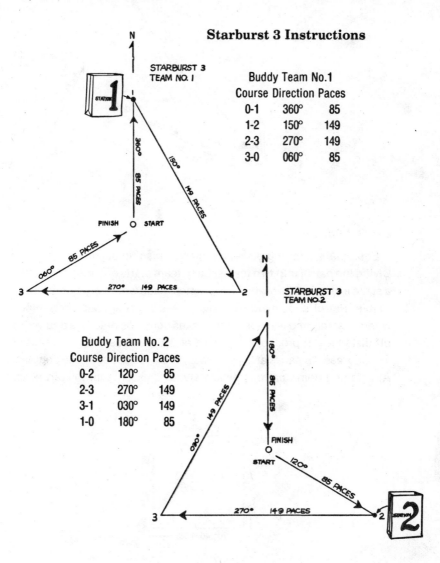

Buddy Team No.1

Course	Direction	Paces
0-1	360°	85
1-2	150°	149
2-3	270°	149
3-0	060°	85

Buddy Team No. 2

Course	Direction	Paces
0-2	120°	85
2-3	270°	149
3-1	030°	149
1-0	180°	85

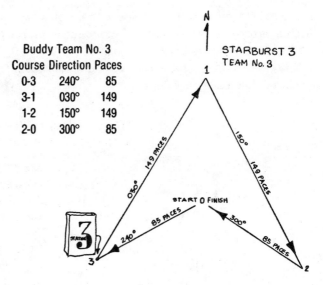

Buddy Team No. 3		
Course	Direction	Paces
0-3	240°	85
3-1	030°	149
1-2	150°	149
2-0	300°	85

Lay Out Square

Equipment. Starting stake, compass, finishing stake.

Divide the patrol into two teams. Each team starts out at a point where a stake is driven down with its top almost flush with the ground, barely visible. Patrol should not be able to see starting stake from place where last reading is made. Patrol takes compass readings and walks off distances. It proceeds 40 paces at 090 degrees, then 40 paces at 180 degrees, 40 paces at 270 degrees, finally 40 paces at 360 degrees. At finishing point, patrol places a stake. Closest team to start wins.

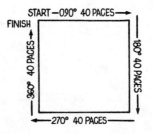

Cents of Direction

Equipment. Magnet for each team, paper clips and pennies.
Teams line up in relay formation facing the opposite end of the room
where a magnet is placed for each team. Each Scout has a penny and a
paper clip. On signal, first Scout runs to magnet; straightens out paper
clip to look like this. Strokes one end of the paper clip with the magnet.
Runs back to team and tags second Scout who repeats the process.
First team to use their cents of direction by balancing the hooked end
of the paper clip on a penny and are facing south wins.

Hold the penny flat between thumbs and forefingers and balance
the end of the paper clip on the penny like this. It will swing into a
north-south line up. Depending on which end of the magnet was used,
the balancing end will be either north or south.

Measurement

Measure a Distance

Equipment. Tape measure, distance computer from *Official Boy Scout Handbook*, pages 574-76.

Select two points to be measured that are more than 30.48 m (100 ft.) apart. Let each Scout pace the distance and determine its length in feet or meters. Check the distance with the tape measure. Scout with the most accurate measurement wins.

Pace Off 50 Meters

Equipment. Tape measure, distance computer from *Official Boy Scout Handbook*, slips of paper and nails.

On a level area let each Scout pace off what he thinks is 50 meters. Scouts should use the same starting line and lane. Each Scout marks the spot he thinks is exactly 50 meters from the starting line with his name on a piece of paper. Paper is anchored in place with a nail. NOTE: 50 meters is 164 feet.

Minute Judging

Equipment. Watch.

Scouts are seated on the floor. Leader looks at watch, says "Go." All the boys try to judge when a minute is over. When a boy thinks the time is up, he rises. Scout to rise closest to exact minute wins. Repeat, using other lengths of time.

Communication

Message Relay

Equipment. For each team, message of 10 or more words, written on paper, then each word cut out separately, and pieces mixed together. Paper, pencil.

Teams line up, opposite a hat containing cut-up message. On signal, Scouts run up, take one word from hat, and bring it back to their partner who is in charge of arranging words into a message. The message orders something done—first team to do it wins.

Message is: "Take off your right shoe and sit on the floor and fold your arms."

Mobilize

Equipment. Mobilization plan.

Your whole patrol is needed in the next 10 minutes! Can you get them together that fast? Here is one way to do it. Set up a call chain like this:

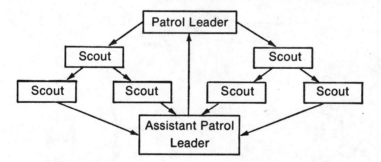

Call two patrol members who in turn call two more members. Then they call your assistant patrol leader who calls you to let you know that each Scout has received the message. Use this system sometime when you need to make a change in the time or place of a meeting. Use the telephone or personal contact.

Silent Fun

Equipment. None.

Patrol leader gives silent signals for formations, one after the other: move forward, hurry, halt, spread out, assemble, attention, etc. Object is for buddy team to follow each signal as quickly as possible. First team to obey a field signal scores 10 points. Team talking or moving with unnecessary noise loses 5 points.

ASSEMBLE

HURRY

FORWARD

SCOUT SIGN

SPREAD OUT

FIST

ATTENTION

HALT

Morse Relay

Equipment. One signal flag or flashlight or blinker for each team. Teams line up in relay formation. On word "Go," first player from each patrol runs up to flag or blinker and sends Morse letter "A." Races back to touch off next player, who runs up, sends "B," returns, and so on, until all letters of the alphabet have been sent. First team to finish with correct letters wins.

Morse Steal the Bacon

Equipment. Buzzer.

Divide patrol into two teams. Use the regular rules for Steal the Bacon, except give pairs on opposing teams letters of the alphabet instead of numbers. The leader sends the letter with a buzzer or flag instead of shouting a number as in the original game. When a boy hears his letter sounded on the buzzer, he runs out to steal the "bacon."

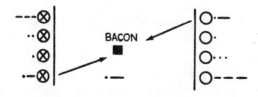

Observation

Object Hunt

Equipment. As needed.

Animal Hunt—Stand a small toy animal somewhere in the room, tell the Scouts to start looking for it, but that each one, as soon as he sees it, is to sit down quietly without giving it away. The fun comes in watching the last ones.

Hunt the Stamp—Played in the same way. Stick a stamp on the troop number of some Scout.

Hunt the Candy—Hide candy, preferably paper wrapped, all over the room. Each Scout upon spying a piece must point his nose at it and give the patrol call, whereupon the patrol leader comes and collects it. Patrol finally eats the candy collected.

The Leaking Backpack

Equipment. As needed. Also paper and pencils.

Game leader arranges various articles not too conspicuously along one side of a path. They may include: Flashlight, toothbrush, soap, toothpaste, stocking, matchbox, spoon, comb, etc. The whole patrol passes slowly along the road in a single file. No one is permitted to walk back when he has passed a certain article. Afterward, Scouts prepare list of articles seen, in right order.

Stalking

Walking Statues

Equipment. None.

Two half-patrol teams start from opposite ends of a room or field, advancing on a leader who stands halfway between them. A team can only advance while the leader is facing the opposite way. He turns around at will, whereupon everyone he faces must be motionless. If he detects the least movement, the guilty party is sent back to the starting line to begin again. This continues until some player reaches the center and touches the leader, thus winning for his team and becoming the next leader.

Crossing the Gap

Equipment. Marker for start and finish.

In broken terrain or underbrush, a course is laid out, about 100 paces long, with starting and finishing points indicated. Two or more observers move along a line parallel to the course, but about 40 paces removed from it, to look for anyone moving along the course. On a signal, the Scouts "hit the dirt" at the starting point, then attempt to creep or crawl, using all natural cover, to the finishing point without being seen by the observers. Set an appropriate time limit for the course. Any boy seen is called to stand up, and remains standing until time is up. First Scout through is the winner.

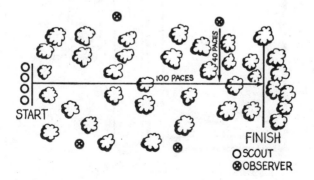

Camping

Pack Relay

Equipment. For each team a pack and all the articles required for a successful overnight camp.

Divide patrol into teams lined up in relay formation opposite empty pack and camping articles. Scout No. 1 runs up, packs first item, runs back, touches off next Scout, who runs up and packs an item, and so on. Team with best-packed pack, with items packed in best order, wins.

Blanket Rolling

Equipment. Two blankets.

Divide patrol into teams. Team lines up in relay formation opposite its blanket. On word "Go," No. 1 runs to the blanket and rolls it up into a tight roll, finishing with "ears" tucked in the roll. Picks up rolled blanket, brings it back to No. 2, who carries the rolled blanket back to the rolling area, where he unrolls it completely and rerolls. Contest continues until all Scouts have rolled and carried the blanket. No straps or strings can be used. Blanket must be secure enough to be picked up and transported without loosening. Team completing first wins.

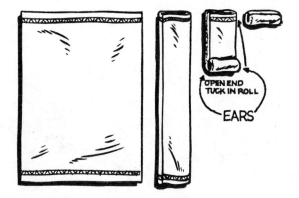

Tent Pitching

Equipment. Four tents with poles and pegs; axes.

Divide patrol into buddy teams. Team lines up with a tent neatly rolled in front of it, poles and pegs enclosed inside of tent. Teams at attention. At command "Go," team sets up its tents. Tents must be neat and tight. When tent is erected, team lines up in front of it at attention. Team finishing first wins.

Flagpole Raising

Equipment. Five Scout staves, one of them with patrol flag attached; eight pieces of heavy cord for four double lashings; three guy ropes, about 5 m (17 ft.) long; three wooden stakes. Hammer for driving stakes.

Patrol against time. Patrol lines up with four Scout staves (or equivalent) and the patrol flag attached to a fifth staff. On signal, Scouts lash the five staves together (patrol flag staff at top) to form pole, approximately 4 paces long. They then attach three guy lines about two-thirds of the way to the top, raise pole, and stake down the guy lines so that pole stands vertically. When finished, patrol forms single line at base of pole, comes to attention. Beat 4 minutes.

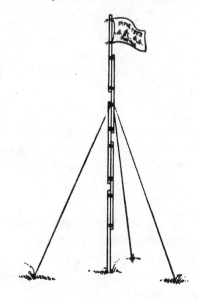

Patrol Menus

On the following pages you'll find food lists and recipes for easy-to-prepare patrol menus.

Now, before you get into the details of these menus, here are a few pointers:

Amounts. The amounts given will feed seven Scouts generously, eight Scouts well. When you use the menus for a patrol of five or six, subtract one-quarter of the amounts where possible. For a patrol of nine or 10, add one-quarter.

Food Buying. We've tried to be very specific about the buying. Bread is given in slices—no two companies seem to cut their bread the same way. For breakfast, we've said "dry cereal only—meaning any of the scores on the market. Pick your own.

You may not always be able to get certain things the food lists call for—so get something else. If you can't get cupcakes, get some other cake. If you can't get fresh fruit, buy canned.

Staples. Every cook knows about certain things that are needed to "polish off" a meal—salt, pepper, vinegar, sugar, mustard, and the like. Most of the time you can't specify the amounts. It's a matter of taste rather than of ounces. The staples are mentioned in the lists to remind you to take them along.

Equipment. The menus can be prepared easily in the Trail Chef Cook Kit, with its 4 pots and 2 pans. You'll also need the following: 1 grater, 1 measuring spoon, 2 large spoons, 1 large pot for heating dishwater (largest pot of Trail Chef Cook Kit will do.)

Preparation. When you use the step-by-step method described in the menus, two Scouts should be able to prepare supper in not more than 60 minutes, breakfast in 30 minutes, and lunch in 30 minutes. But notice the reminder at *every* meal: *Read TWICE before starting.*

Hike and Trail Foods

Dehydrated and freeze-dried foods are popular because they are lightweight, take up little space, and require no refrigeration. To many hikers that's worth the extra money these foods cost.

Fortunately, suitable trail foods are on your supermarket shelves. They are produced for everyone—not just hikers—and so, are less expensive. Shop around. Look for foods in burnable pouches. Avoid cans and bottles that must be carried out. Keep in mind that easy-to-prepare foods, which do not require a lot of cooking time, are usually better for a trek.

In the summer and fall, when fruits and vegetables are plentiful, try drying your own hike foods. Ask your county agricultural agent for information on using a solar oven. This could be a good patrol and troop project.

In the meantime, watch for bargains in your supermarkets. Here are some common foods to choose from:

Dehydrated baked beans	Dried chipped beef
Dried beans	Raisins, dates, figs, peaches, apricots
Dried potatoes	
Dried tomato paste	Instant puddings
Instant soup	Instant cereals
Breakfast bars	Beef jerky
Pop tarts	Bacon bits
Scrambled egg mix	Nuts
Squeeze cheese	Crackers or wafers
Health foods	Drink crystals
Pancake mixes	Powdered milk
Bouillon cubes and gravy mix	Chocolate milk mix
	Biscuit mixes

Check packages for quantities needed to feed your patrol. Do some experimenting at home to learn how to prepare these foods, and you'll be better prepared to use them on the trail.

Patrol Menu No. 1

SUPPER: Marco Polo Dinner

Carrot and Cabbage Slaw

Spaghetti and Meatballs

Bread and Butter   Milk and Fruit Drink

Butterscotch Pudding

UTENSILS: 4 pots, 2 frying pans, 1 vegetable grater

FOOD LIST:

1½ lbs. spaghetti	16 slices bread
2 lbs. chopped beef	¼ lb. butter or margarine
2 medium-size onions	3 boxes instant
1 No. 2½ can tomatoes	butterscotch pudding
1 No. 1 can tomato soup	1 qt. milk
3 tbsp. shortening	2 pkgs. fruit drink
2 fresh carrots	powder (for 1 gal.)
1 small cabbage	sugar, salt, pepper
1 tall can evaporated milk	

PREPARATION: Read TWICE before starting.

1. Prepare the butterscotch pudding according to the instructions on the boxes with this exception: Use tall can evaporated milk and 4 cups water, instead of ordinary milk. Set aside to thicken.

2. Peel onions and slice fine. Roll meat into small balls.

3. Put 1½ tbsp. shortening in each frying pan. When hot, put in the meatballs, half of them in each pan. Let them brown a little, then add the sliced onions. When the onions are light brown, pour in tomatoes and tomato soup, half for each pan. Finally, add 1 tsp. sugar and ½ tsp. salt to each pan. Place on back of fire to simmer.

4. When the water is boiling furiously, add the broken-up spaghetti. Cook vigorously for about 10 minutes until soft, but not mushy.

5. To make carrot and cabbage slaw, wash and scrape carrots and grate them. Cut the cabbage in halves, then in quarters, then in eighths. Grate on the coarse grater. Discard the core. Mix the grated cabbage and carrots in a pot.

6. When spaghetti is done, carefully pour off the boiling water. Don't pour out the spaghetti. Mix tomato sauce and meatballs with spaghetti.

7. Follow instructions on package for fruit drink.

8. Serve pudding.

BREAKFAST: French Toast Feast

Sliced Oranges	French Toast	Cereal
Syrup and Jam	Bread and Butter	Cocoa and Milk

UTENSILS: 3 pot, 2 frying pans

FOOD LIST:

10 medium-size oranges	¼ lb. butter or margarine
8 individual dry cereal	1 1-pt. bottle syrup
4 eggs	1 8-oz. jar jam
1 tall can evaporated milk	¼ lb. ready-to-use cocoa
24 slices bread	2 qts. milk
4 tbsp. shortening	sugar

PREPARATION: Read TWICE before starting.
1. Put on 9 to 10 cups of water to boil for cocoa.
2. Peel and slice the oranges thin into a pot. Sprinkle with sugar.
3. For French toast, beat four eggs in a pot with a fork, and add one tall can evaporated milk and an equal amount of water.
4. Quickly dip (do not soak) the slices of bread in this mixture and fry them in hot pans that have been greased with a piece of clean paper dipped in shortening. Fry on both sides until brown. Watch carefully as French toast browns quickly. Serve with syrup, jam, or sugar as desired.
5. When ready, pour boiling water over 2 heaping tsp. of ready-to-use cocoa in each camper's cup. Stir well.

LUNCH: Klondike Kold Kut Snack

Sliced Tomatoes	Cold Cut Sandwiches	Bread, Butter, and Jelly
	Fresh Fruit Salad	Milk

UTENSILS: 1 pot

FOOD LIST:

½ lb. sliced meat	1 8-oz. jar jelly
½ lb. sliced bologna	3 qts. milk
½ lb. sliced liverwurst	3 apples
6 tomatoes (about 1½ lbs.)	4 bananas
32 slices bread	3 oranges
¼ lb. butter or margarine	sugar, salt, pepper

PREPARATION: Read TWICE before starting.
1. Make up 16 sandwiches from cold cuts—meat, bologna, liverwurst, or other cold cuts. Cut in halves, to make four halves for each camper.
2. Wash tomatoes well and cut out stem end. Slice thin and serve.
3. To make fruit salad, peel the fruit. Cut the oranges, apples, bananas into small pieces, dropping them into pot. Sprinkle with sugar and serve cold for dessert.

Patrol Menu No. 2

SUPPER: Hong Kong Surprise

Chow Mein and Boiled Rice

Bread and Butter

Milk and Fruit Drink

Peaches and Cookies

UTENSILS: 2 pots, 2 frying pans

FOOD LIST:

1½ lbs. stew meat	¼ lb. butter or margarine
2 medium-size onions	2 pkgs. fruit drink powder
1 small bunch celery	(for 1 gal.)
1 small cabbage (1½ lbs.)	2 qts. milk
1 14-oz. box (4 cups)	16 fresh peaches or
instant rice	2 No. 2 cans
1 small bottle soy sauce	1 1-lb. box cookies
1 tbsp. shortening	sugar, salt, pepper
16 slices bread	

PREPARATION: Read TWICE before starting.

1. Peel onions and slice thin. Break the celery apart, wash each piece, and chop into small pieces. Slice the cabbage thin. Cut the meat into small strips.

2. Put 1 qt. water in a pot for the rice (measure with measuring cup or milk bottle). Add 2 level tsp. salt. Bring to a boil. Stir in the rice. Cover. Take the pot off the fire. Let stand 5 minutes. Fluff the rice with a fork.

3. Put 1 tbsp. shortening in one frying pan. When it is hot, put in beef strips and brown them a little. Now add ½ tsp. salt, 1 cup water, and 4 tsp. soy sauce. Divide the meat evenly into two pans and add half of the onions, celery, and cabbage to each pan. Simmer gently over a low fire until meat is tender (about ½ hour). If sauce begins to cook away, add a little more water and stir. When done, serve over boiled rice.

4. Follow instructions for fruit drink.

5. Serve peaches, cookies, and milk.

BREAKFAST: Sunny-Side Up Day Breaker

Stewed Prunes	Fried Eggs	Cereal
Cocoa and Milk	Bread, Butter, and Jam	

UTENSILS: 1 pot, 2 frying pans

FOOD LIST:

1 No. 2½ can stewed dried prunes	¼ lb. butter or margarine
8 individual dry cereal	1 8-oz. jar jam
10 eggs	¼ lb. ready-to-use cocoa
2 tbsp. shortening	2 qts. milk
24 slices bread	sugar, salt, pepper

PREPARATION: Read TWICE before starting.
1. Put on 9 to 10 cups water to boil for cocoa.
2. Open can or jar of prunes. Serve as is.
3. Heat 1 tbsp. shortening in each pan, put in eggs. Fry gently until whites are firm.
4. When ready, pour boiling water over 2 heaping tsp. ready-to-use cocoa in each camper's cup. Stir well.

LUNCH: Napoleon's Secret Weapon

Canned Meat and Lettuce Sandwiches

Peanut Butter and Jelly Sandwiches

Applesauce and Milk

UTENSILS: None

FOOD LIST:

2 12-oz. cans of pressed meat	32 slices bread
1 head lettuce	¼ lb. butter or margarine
1 8-oz. jar peanut butter	3 qts. milk
1 8-oz. glass jelly	1 No. 2 can applesauce
	salt, pepper, mustard

PREPARATION: Read TWICE before starting.
1. Wash lettuce and separate leaves.
2. Cut pressed meat into thin slices and place on bread for eight sandwiches. Add lettuce leaf to each sandwich. Spread on a little mustard if desired or put jar on table for self-service.
3. Make eight peanut butter and jelly sandwiches. Cut all sandwiches in halves, to make four halves for each camper.
4. Serve applesauce.

Patrol Menu No. 3

SUPPER: Red Baron's Delight

Mashed Potatoes

Hot Dogs and Sauerkraut

Bread and Butter

Milk and Fruit Drink   Chocolate Pudding

UTENSILS: 4 pots

FOOD LIST:

16 hot dogs (about 2 lbs.)	3 boxes chocolate
1 No. 2½ can sauerkraut	pudding powder
1 6½ oz. package	1 tall can evaporated milk
instant mashed potatoes	2 qts. milk
16 slices bread	2 pkgs. fruit drink powder
¼ lb. butter or margarine	mustard, sugar, salt, pepper

PREPARATION: Read TWICE before starting.

1. Prepare the chocolate pudding according to the instructions on the boxes, with this exception: Use 1 tall can of evaporated milk and 4 cups of water, instead of the milk amount given in the directions. Put aside to thicken.

2. Wash the hot dogs and place them in a pot with enough water to cover them. Bring to boil, then simmer gently for 5 to 8 minutes. Drain. Pour in sauerkraut and heat together.

3. Pour into a medium-size pot 1½ cups water and ½ cup milk. Add ½ tsp. salt and 1 tbsp. butter. Bring to a boil. Remove pot from the fire. Stir in the instant mashed potatoes using a fork. Whip with the fork until fluffy.

4. Follow instructions on package for making fruit drink.

5. Serve pudding.

BREAKFAST: Flapjack Day Starter

Grapefruit Juice   Pancakes and Syrup   Cereal

Bread, Butter, and Jam   Cocoa and Milk

UTENSILS: 2 1-gal. pots, 2 frying pans

FOOD LIST:

2 No. 2 cans grapefruit juice	¼ lb. butter or margarine
8 individual dry cereal	1 1-pt. bottle syrup
1 pkg. pancake flour	1 8-oz. jar jam
(about 20 oz.)	16 slices bread
1 tall can evaporated milk	2 qts. milk
3 tbsp. shortening	sugar

PREPARATION: Read TWICE before starting.

1. Put on 9 to 10 cups of water to boil for cocoa.

2. To make pancake batter, follow instructions on the box, using evaporated milk diluted with same amount of water instead of fresh milk, and adding 2 tsp. sugar. Be careful not to make the batter too thin. Heat both frying pans and grease them with clean paper dipped in shortening.

3. Pour a tablespoon of batter on the hot pans for each pancake. When bubbles start to break around the edge, turn cakes over and fry on other side. Serve with syrup, jam, or sugar as desired.

4. When ready, pour boiling water over 2 heaping tsp. ready-to-use cocoa in each camper's cup. Stir well.

LUNCH: Energy Combo

Cheese Sandwiches   Lettuce and Tomato Sandwiches
Chocolate Milk   Vegetable-Tomato Soup   Oatmeal Cookies

UTENSILS: 2 pots

FOOD LIST:

3 pkgs. vegetable-tomato	32 slices bread
soup mix	¼ lb. butter or margarine
¾ lb. sliced cheese	3 qts. milk
4 tomatoes (about 1 lb.)	1 1-lb. box oatmeal cookies
1 head lettuce	salt, pepper
1 1-pt. can chocolate syrup	

PREPARATION: Read TWICE before starting.

1. Make soup according to instructions on package.

2. Use two slices cheese, lettuce leaf for each of eight cheese sandwiches.

3. Wash tomatoes, remove stem ends, and slice thin. Place tomato slices on bread and add a leaf of lettuce. Make eight sandwiches. Cut all sandwiches in half, to make four halves for each camper.

4. Follow instructions on can of chocolate syrup to make chocolate milk.

5. Serve cookies.

Campfire Ideas

Songs

Singing has always been a favorite activity in Scouting. It's fun to sing a marching song on the road or join voices around the campfire after a good day at camp. Your attitude will have a lot to do with how your patrol likes singing. Realize that while it may take a little while to teach your gang the words and melody to a song, it's worth the effort. A singing patrol is a fun patrol.

To teach a song, sing it by yourself a couple of times so the rest of the patrol picks up the tune and words. Spend extra time making sure that your Scouts know the words. Start singing together softly. Let your patrol begin to enjoy singing together—they'll want to sing more and more.

It's fun to try to match a song to the mood of the moment. "Hi-Ho! Nobody Home" would be a great choice for singing at the start of a patrol hike. "Shenandoah" would be nice around the glowing embers of the campfire, while "Taps" would bring the day to a close. The key is to teach your group enough songs so they will be able to find one to fit your special moments. Try the *Boy Scout Songbook*, No. 3224.

Yells

Making noise is a favorite sport of Scout-age boys—so why not direct their enthusiasm into yelling? It's fun, and what's more important, really builds up patrol spirit. Before a hike or a skit, or any time it won't bother others, let the patrol give a yell. It'll knit your group together and release some excess energy.

Try to get one of your Scouts to be your cheermaster. His job is leading the patrol in yells and cheers. He should know several, teach them to the patrol, and direct the actual yelling of the cheers. Pick a patrol member with lots of spirit. He'll probably be glad to help out.

You might want to make up your own patrol yell. "Buffalo - Buffalo - we're in line, Buffalo - Buffalo - rain or shine, Go Buffalo!" You can make up special yells for special occasions.

American Scout Yell
A-M-E-R-I-C-A
Boy Scouts, Boy Scouts
U.S.A.!

B-B-B-O-Y!
B-B! B-O-Y! S-S! S-C-O
U-U! U-T-S! Boy Scouts of America! *(repeat)*

We Are Boy Scouts!
We are Boy Scouts! *(pause)*
We know what we're about *(pause)*
Come to see and come to do! *(pause)*
Betcha we'll have fun with you!

Locomotive Cheer
Starts slowly:
    B--O--Y--S--C--O--U--T....
Then faster:
    B-O-Y-S-C-O-U-T....
Gradually faster:
B-O-Y-S-C-O-U-T---Yea Boy Scouts!

Good Turn Yell

Leader:	Patrol
Do you do a Good Turn?	*(shout):* We do a Good Turn!
Do you do a Good Turn?	*(shout):* We do a Good Turn!
When? *(pause)*	*(shout):* EVERY DAY—HEY!

Scout Law Yell
(Shouted quickly and sharply)
A Scout is
Trustworthy, Loyal, Helpful,
Friendly, Courteous, Kind,
Obedient, Cheerful, Thrifty,
Brave, Clean, and Reverent!

Hand Claps

Hand claps are used for special recognition. If a member of your patrol has just qualified for First Class, or if a father has just given an excellent presentation on the First Aid merit badge, a clap is in order. The highest honor a Scout or guest can receive is the "Class A" clap. It is done in perfect time. It goes 1-2-3-4, 1-2-, 1-2-, 1-2-3-4, 1-2, 1-2, 1-2-3-4, 1-2-3-4, 1. There should be dead silence after the last clap. The Class B clap is exactly the same except that on the final clap the hands miss each other. A third variation is the Class C clap, which is the same as a Class B clap except that the hands come together on the "second try" on the final clap. Make up your own patrol variation. If a skit or stunt does not rate a "Class A" or patrol clap it might be a good idea to try one of these novelty claps instead.

Catsup bottle. One hand is clenched into a fist and is struck with the palm of the other hand against the thumb and forefinger of the fist as if trying to force catsup out of a bottle.

Freight train. The applause simulates a freight train in the distance, approaching the station, and then fading off again into the distance. This is a four-beat handclap with the first beat of each grouping of four made much louder than the following three beats. The clever leader can speed up, slow down, stop, start, and speed up again by varying the tempo. Throw in a few train whistle sound effects to add to the fun.

Clam. Each Scout holds up one hand and makes a sound by bringing the fingers of this hand down quickly on the palm of the same hand, much as a clam in opening and closing its shell. This, of course, is something less than deafening.

Barber. One hand, palm up, becomes the razor strop and the other hand the razor. The sound is made as the hand simulating the razor is moved back and forth across the other hand that is representing the strop.

Rain. Clapping hands very fast with the tempo of falling rain, the leader slowly raises his hands well above his head. With hands low, the clapping is very, very soft, hardly audible. As the hands are raised higher, the group finally reaches a wild handclap applause. Then the rain dies away to complete silence as the hands are lowered.

Catch-on Games

Games are another part of the campfire. It's important to keep the right spirit during "catch-on" games. It's fun for each boy to learn the trick, but it's no fun when some boys think they are being made fun of. Sometimes it's a good idea to go around several times and then stop, keeping the game or trick for next time. Try some of these favorites:

This is the moon. Secretly tip off the patrol leaders' council on how this game works, so you'll have help in playing.

The leader takes a stick in his hand, steps to the center of the campfire area, and clears his throat. He then draws a circle on the ground with the stick. He puts in two dots for eyes, one dot the nose, and a line for the mouth, saying as he does this, "This is the 'moon.' It has two eyes, a nose, and a mouth." He then challenges Scouts around the circle to do it exactly as he did. Each Scout in turn, including members of the patrol leaders' council, steps forward and tries to copy the exact motions of the leader. As each Scout finishes, the leader says "right" or "wrong." The trick, of course, is for the Scout to clear his throat before drawing the "moon." Keep trying until all Scouts catch on. As more and more get the idea, it becomes very humorous as they exaggerate the clearing of the throat as they come up for their turn, and yet some of the boys are still unable to get the trick.

Jack's alive. Put one end of a stick (or a cork fastened to a stick) into the fire until it starts to burn. Put out the flame, leaving a glowing ember. Start the stick at one point in the circle of Scouts. Each Scout must blow once on the ember and pass the stick to the boy on his left, saying "Jack's alive" as he does. The ember stick is moved rapidly around the circle until it finally dies out. When the ember dies, the Scout who is holding the stick at the time drops out. Relight the stick and start again.

20 questions. One Scout thinks of an object familiar to the rest of the troop. In turn around the circle, Scouts ask questions (one for each turn) that can be answered by a simple yes or no. Object may be identified by presenter of idea as animal, vegetable, or mineral before questioning beings. The Scout who finally makes the correct guess as to the identity of the object becomes the one to think of an object for the next round. While the title of the game is 20 Questions, don't restrict it to this number, but rather let it continue until the object is identified.

Crossed and uncrossed. Secretly tip off the patrol leaders' council on how this game works, so you'll have help in playing.

The troop is seated in a circle around the fire. The leader starts the game with a stick in each hand. He passes the two sticks to the Scout on his right with the sticks either crossed or held apart uncrossed. When handing them, he says, "I pass these crossed" (if his legs, not the sticks, are crossed; if his legs were uncrossed he would say, "I pass these uncrossed"). The Scout on his right, if he catches on or knows the game says, "I receive these crossed" (if his legs are crossed). He then might uncross his legs and pass the sticks to the next player to his right saying, "I pass these uncrossed."

On each receipt or pass, the leader should say "right" or "wrong." Remember, the position of the sticks has nothing to do with the words. All that is involved is the position of the legs.

Keep playing until all Scouts catch on.

Skits

Skits take the longest to prepare and are perhaps the most entertaining part of a campfire. A good skit by your patrol can really help out a program. The key to a funny skit is to just relax and play around. Don't be afraid to really ham it up.

There are some basics in song and skit preparation. The first, which seems obvious enough, is that the leader should have a solid idea of what he is going to do. If he is leading a skit, he should know it well, all the lines, the plot, and what effect he wants to achieve. After the leader is secure in his own preparation, he should "walk through" the skit or stunt while feeding the actors their lines and mimicking their expressions. The group should try several practice runs. Remember, practice makes perfect; you didn't learn how to build a fire in 1 day, and you won't be expert skit masters overnight either. With relaxed practice, however, you will improve steadily. Soon the day will come when other patrol leaders will ask you, "How do you get your gang to put on such great skits?"

Don't be caught flat-footed when a troop campfire is coming up. You know your patrol is going to be called on, so be prepared. Scrounge around for skit ideas. TV variety shows, jokes, riddles, and *Boys' Life* are all fertile grounds for new skit ideas. Practice your favorite skits around your patrol campfire in order to get them ready for the troop or council campfire. Props need not be elaborate. In fact, they shouldn't be. A fair-size piece of log can be a rifle, a Scout neckerchief a lady's bonnet, and a bit of sooty smudge on the cheek can be whiskers. Have fun with it. Then, when it's your turn, Go! Enjoy putting on skits and your troop will enjoy watching. Here are some skit ideas.

Shorties

Shorties are quick skits. They are usually funny "one liners" with plenty of action. They are used in between longer skits and songs in a campfire program. As a patrol is preparing their skit, a Scout runs across the stage area. "It's all around me, it's all around me!" he screams hysterically. "What is it?" asks a voice from the crowd. "Air," the actor replies calmly. Here are some others.

Why are you pulling that rope? A Scout calmly walks across the stage area pulling a rope behind him. Just as he is about to leave, a friend from the crowd asks, "Why are you pulling that rope?" "Ever tried pushing one?" the Scout replies.

Kung Fu master. The patrol leader brings up the smallest (youngest) boy in the patrol and declares that the boy is a red belt Kung Fu master. He can do his whole exercise of kicks and deadly jabs in the blink of an eye. "Wanna see it?" asks the patrol leader. The young Scout remains perfectly still. "Wanna see it again?" asks the patrol leader. "If you blinked, you missed it!"

Be Prepared. A Scout wearing a First Class badge walks across the stage area. Another Scout stops him—"Not so fast there, let's check on some of your Scout skills. What's a council fire? "Dunno," answers the lad. "Well then, what's the Napoleon method for estimating distances?" "Uh, beats me, sir." "Let's try first aid skills, then. What would you do if I were bleeding from an artery in my leg?" "Mister, I'm afraid you would bleed to death, this is my brother's shirt."

Scout Law. In this activity the senior patrol leader assigns a point of the Scout Law to each patrol. The patrol invents a little skit to demonstrate that part of the Scout Law in action. A patrol given "A Scout is reverent" might show a family attending church. The patrol given "A Scout is brave" might depict a rescue attempt. The audience tries to guess which point of the Scout Law they are acting out. A variation is to have the patrols pantomime the skits.

TV commercials. Do a takeoff on a TV commercial. A popular skit is "Sudsy-Dudsy Laundry Soap," where a pitchman demonstrates the cleaning and freshening qualities of his product. He washes various items in a Scout's wardrobe in his tub filled with the soap, repeating— "sudsy-dudsy, sudsy-dudsy, sudsy-dudsy," as he washes. He smells each item and says "(snif)...ah—Sudsy-Dudsy." Finally he washes a pair of Scout socks, smells them, and returns them to the tub, saying— "sudsy-dudsy, sudsy-dudsy, sudsy-dudsy...."

Bible tableau. In "Bible Tableau" each patrol is told to make themselves into a "statue" depicting a scene from scripture. Once they get into position, they cannot move or say anything. The audience tries to guess the biblical scene that the patrol is depicting. Examples of tableaus are Moses crossing the sea (Scouts in two files facing each other with their hands up and patrol leader pretending to hold up a staff between them) and Noah and the ark (Scouts lined up two by two as if they are going up a plank as patrol leader looks on).

Worst aid. A group of hiking Scouts happens across a "victim" who has just sprained his ankle. They make fumbling attempts to help him, but only succeed in hurting him more by stepping on his leg, hitting him on the head, accidentally kicking him, putting a tourniquet on his neck, etc. Finally the "victim" runs away. The patrol leader turns to the audience and comments, "Humph, that's gratitude for you."

Skit bag. Each patrol is given a "skit bag," prepared beforehand. The skit bags, one for each patrol, contain old articles of clothing, hats, and assorted throwaways. Each patrol must make up a skit that uses each prop in their bag. This skit idea develops creativity and dramatic talent.

Talent show. Each patrol must put on one act, either as a group or by sending up an individual to perform. The patrol might teach a song, put on a skit, teach or put on a trick, or ask one of their members to tell a story, do a trick, or perform some other entertainment. This gives a chance for patrols and individuals to display and be recognized for their talents.

Storytelling

Many boys enjoy hearing a good story around the campfire, yet it seems that few boys want to get up and do it. As a result, most guys think that it's just too hard to tell a story. Television and other audiovisual bombardment have made boys used to "professional" entertainment. In former times, a good storyteller was always popular, just the guy to relieve the boredom of the dreary tasks of the day. Camp-outs capture part of the frontier spirit, and you'll find that Scouts will not only sit through but greatly enjoy a well-told story. Revive the art of storytelling in your patrol.

The first step is to select a good story. Good stories for campfire storytelling are hard to come by. "Casey at the Bat" and "The Cremation of Sam McGee" have been used successfully. O. Henry's short stories work well. Ask the storytellers at your district camporee; chances are they would be happy to help out.

Once a story is selected, read it over at least three times. Then try to relate the story in your own words. Speak out loud and don't mind that you are a bit thin on detail at this point. Go back over the story, trying to remember items that you missed. Then tell the story to yourself again. Once you are comfortable that you know the story, try to liven it up. Picture the events and characters of the story in your mind. Retell it in front of a mirror. Now you're ready to tell the story to your patrol.

The main thing needed to be a storyteller is courage. Courage to try. You might just be surprised at how much your group enjoys it.

Projects

Your flying colors. Your patrol will want a flag of its own—one you can take along wherever you go. When you take part in a game or contest, keep it posted for all to see. When you hike the trails, carry it with you and hold it high. Appoint a Scout to be the flagbearer and rotate the job so that every fellow has his chance to carry it. At troop meetings, in camp, and on all other activities, make a point to post your flag at the head of the patrol. It's your emblem.

You can enlarge any patrol design easily. Just mark some check points on a grid and connect them with an outline as shown. But you may already have a flag and it may look like this. Or it may have one of the designs shown on the next two pages. If it does, use the grid system to make enlargements for decorating your equipment and furniture.

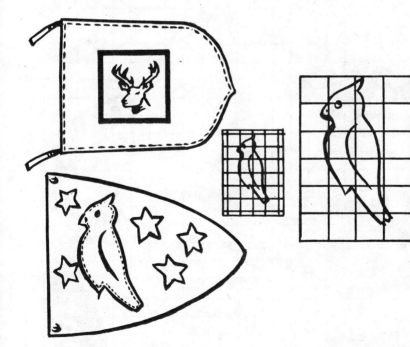

Alligator

Bison

Flying Eagle

Antelope

Bobcat

Fox

Badger

Bobwhite

Frog

Bat

Cobra

Frontiersman

Bear

Eagle

Beaver

Flaming Arrow

Hawk

Indian

Pheasant

Roadrunner

Liberty

Pine Tree

Stag

Moose

Raccoon

Tiger

Owl

Ram

Viking

Panther

Rattlesnake

Pedro

Raven

Wolf

You may want to design your own flag. One way to do that is to run an "art" contest. Divide the patrol into buddy teams, have each team develop a design, then vote for the best. After you have decided on the shape and design, get a piece of material—something strong and tough like leather, plastic, canvas, duck or sailcloth. Transfer the design to the material; then paint it or get a patrol mother to embroider it. Or cut out the design from a piece of material of a contrasting color and cement it on with textile cement. Or make a stencil of your patrol emblem that could also serve to decorate your tents, packs, and other gear. Add a binding or hem to your flag and reinforce the corner holes with grommets. Then get a sturdy staff and tie your flag to it with leather thongs or shoelaces.

Whatever you put on it should have a special meaning to every member so that he can take pride in it—and in his patrol. For example, the Blister Busters got their name on their first hike. Your patrol flag can build patrol spirit.

Build a flag stand. As a final step in making your own patrol flag, you need to build a stand to hold your proud emblem. Cut the parts from dry seasoned wood. The two end pieces are plywood and the others can be any sturdy wood of the right thickness. Secure all the parts together with screws or nails.

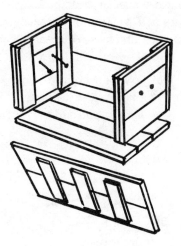

A patrol chest. You can make this useful patrol chest easily out of pine boards or any available soft lumber. You can make up your own dimensions, but a chest 3 feet long with ends that are 2 feet square is about the right size. For this, 1x12s and 1x8s are best. Seal the seams with an all-purpose glue and insert flat-headed wood screws to hold the box rigid. Drill small holes for the screws and countersink the heads to maintain the smooth surface. Make sure your hinges are large enough to do the job. Use plenty of sandpaper to get rid of the rough edges. Then give your patrol chest a couple coats of paint, stain, or shellac—or, if you prefer, just leave it in its natural wood. The rope handles enable you to shift the chest around; it isn't designed to be toted long distances. Finally add the hasp and use a padlock to keep your equipment secure. Wood cleats could be added to the bottom.

Adaptable patrol corners, formed by movable panels, produce the right Scouting atmosphere at troop meetings. After the meeting, the panels can be folded back against the wall or removed and stacked in a narrow storage area. The room has a unified feeling, but there is plenty of variation. Each patrol corner looks different and there are various ways to arrange the panels. This phase of interior decorating is a troop function. But the design of each patrol corner is up to each patrol. This is where lots of enthusiasm coupled with some strong imagination comes in handy. Have your patrol members brainstorm for ideas. When their patrol corner becomes their creation, they'll do a better job.

Construct and erect the walls for your patrol corners in the same way you would assemble stage properties. Build the frames out of 1- by 3-inch boards. Cover them with beaverboard, canvas, or plywood and then reinforce the corners and crosspieces with plywood wedges or a T-plate. Add the extra triangles, as shown to use when binding the sides as you set up the partitions. The binding begins and ends at the cleats attached to the opposite corners of the two frames. With this system, the partitions can be taken apart and stored easily. The final step is to decorate the smooth sides of the panels according to your theme.

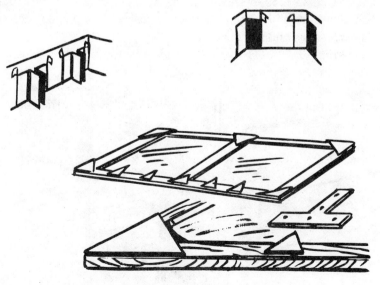

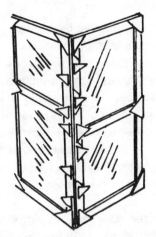

The storage bench in your patrol corner serves as a convenient chest to keep all kinds of patrol equipment. Make it as long as the width of the wall behind it. And you can steady that panel by attaching it to your bench with some screws. Leave room for the back edge of the top to move down when you raise the lid. Build the bench out of plywood or any suitable scrap lumber. Paint it to agree with the design of your patrol corner. Add a hasp if you want to keep the chest locked when you are away. Use it for the things you need for troop meetings such as some rope, a shoeshine kit, handbooks, and merit badge pamphlets. It's a good place to put any gear related to your troop or patrol projects and activities.

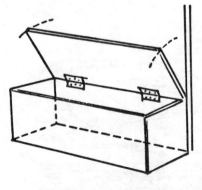

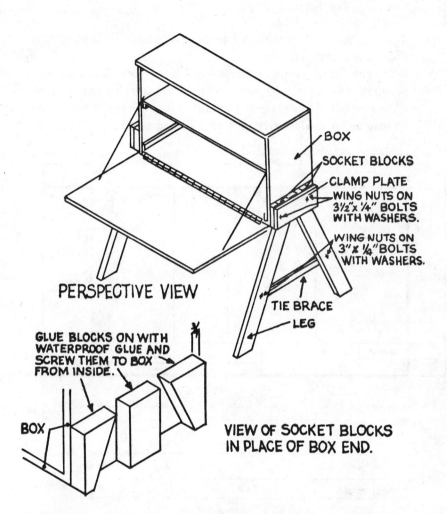

BOX

SOCKET BLOCKS

CLAMP PLATE

WING NUTS ON
3½"x ¼" BOLTS
WITH WASHERS.

WING NUTS ON
3" x ¼" BOLTS
WITH WASHERS.

TIE BRACE

LEG

PERSPECTIVE VIEW

GLUE BLOCKS ON WITH
WATERPROOF GLUE AND
SCREW THEM TO BOX
FROM INSIDE.

BOX

**VIEW OF SOCKET BLOCKS
IN PLACE OF BOX END.**

Patrol food chest. Camping with this food chest provides protection for your food. With the lid open, it becomes a table top on which to prepare your meals.

To assemble the chest, attach the tie braces to the legs, but do not tighten the wing nuts. Loosen the wing nuts on the clamp plates which remain on the outside of the chest. Insert legs in the sockets and tighten the wing nuts. Then tighten the tie brace wing nuts.

When camp is over, loosen the wing nuts on the clamp plates and remove the legs. Tighten the wing nuts on the clamp plates and leave them on the outside of the box. Remove the tie braces and store them and the legs inside the box.

The chest can be made from one 4 by 8 foot sheet of ¾-inch exterior plywood. See cut-out diagram. Paint the chest inside and out with enamel or line the inside with plastic or other washable material. The lid may be lined with hardboard for a cutting surface.

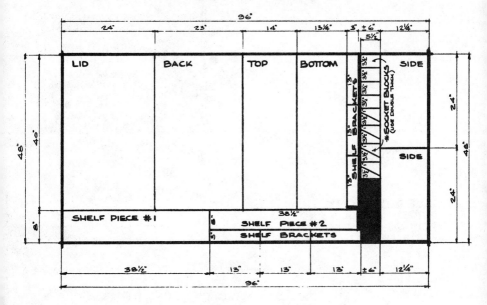

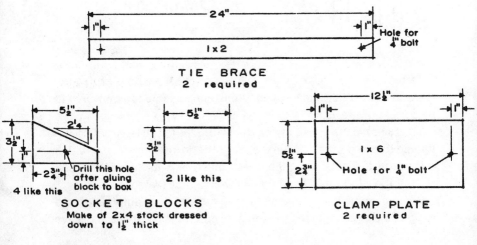

TIE BRACE
2 required

SOCKET BLOCKS
Make of 2x4 stock dressed
down to 1½" thick

CLAMP PLATE
2 required

196

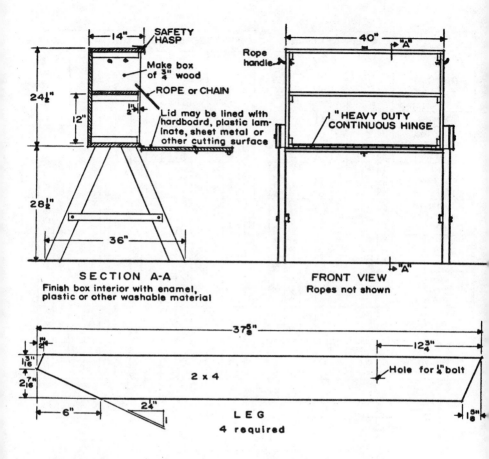

SECTION A-A
Finish box interior with enamel,
plastic or other washable material

FRONT VIEW
Ropes not shown

Patrol equipment may be stored in the food chest when you are not in camp.

A patrol food box is a real asset in a permanent camp. Your patrol cooking gear and staple foods can be stored and carried in the box, and when you set up your camp kitchen you have ready-made storage shelves and work counter. When you're going out for only a weekend camp, or traveling light, take what you need out of the box, and carry these items in your packsacks.

PATROL CHART — SCOUTS ▶

Legend: ● RED—GET GOING ◉ GREEN—KEEP GOING ○ GOLD—GOOD GOING

	PL MIKE 1	2	3	APL TODD 1	2	3	CARLOS 1	2	3	JIM 1	2	3	BOB 1	2	3	TIM 1	2	3	AL 1	2	3	MARK 1	2	3
ON TIME FOR PATROL MEETING	◉◉◉	◉◉◉		◉◉◉	◉◉◉		●●●	◉◉◉		◉◉◉	◉◉◉		◉◉◉	◉◉◉		●●●	◉◉◉		●●●	●◉◉		●●●	◉◉◉	
ON TIME FOR TROOP MEETING	◉◉◉◉	◉◉◉◉		◉◉◉◉	◉◉◉◉		●◉◉○	◉◉◉◉		◉◉◉◉	◉◉◉◉		◉◉◉◉	◉◉◉◉		◉◉●◉	◉◉◉◉		●◉●◉	◉◉◉◉		●◉◉◉	◉◉◉●	
UNIFORM AT TROOP MEETING	◉◉◉◉	◉◉◉◉		◉◉◉◉	◉◉◉◉		●◉◉◉	◉◉◉◉		◉◉◉◉	◉◉◉◉		◉◉◉◉	◉◉◉◉		◉◉●◉	◉◉◉◉		◉◉●◉	◉◉◉◉		●◉◉◉	◉◉◉◉	
DUES PAID	◉◉◉◉	◉◉◉◉		◉◉◉◉	◉◉◉◉		●◉◉◉	◉◉◉◉		◉◉◉◉	◉◉◉◉		◉◉◉◉	◉◉◉◉		◉◉◉◉	◉◉◉●		◉◉◉●	◉◉◉●		●◉◉◉	◉◉◉◉	
ON TIME FOR OUTING	◉	◉		◉	◉		◉	◉		◉	◉		◉	◉		●	◉		◉	◉		◉	◉	
GOOD TURNS	◉	◉		○	○		◉	◉		◉	○		○	○		●	◉		◉	◉		●	◉	
ADVANCEMENT	◉	◉		◉	○		●	◉		●	◉		○	○		●	◉		●	◉		●	◉	

Strategy With Stars or Something

There's magic in a wall chart. Set a chart up with each Scout's name listed and the categories of achievement. Put a star or a gummed dot on the chart whenever a Scout earns it. Such a chart can be the center of patrol interest. You can keep the chart yourself, or better still, ask a Scout to keep it for the whole patrol.

Maybe you can find a way to recognize individual Scouts like football players who wear stars on their helmets for big plays. "We want this patrol to be the best!"

Baden-Powell Patrol Requirements

1. **Spirit.** Have a patrol flag and rally around it. Put your patrol design on equipment. Use your yell or cheer and patrol call. Keep patrol records up to date for 3 months.

2. **Patrol meetings.** Hold two patrol meetings each month for 3 months.

3. **Hikes, outdoor activities, and other events.** Take part in one of these within 3 months.

4. **Good Turns or service projects.** Do two patrol leaders' council approved Good Turns or service projects within 3 months.

5. **Advancement.** Help two patrol members advance one rank during 3 months.

6. **Membership.** Build patrol to full strength (eight Scouts).

7. **Uniform.** Wear the uniform correctly (at least six Scouts).

8. **Patrol leaders' council.** Represent the patrol during three patrol leaders' council meetings within 3 months.

If your patrol measures up to these eight standards for 3 months, every member may wear the B-P star below his patrol medallion. Every 3 months you can earn another star. You can be more than a one-star patrol!

INDEX

A

Advancement, patrol, 20; wall chart, 198

American Scout yell, 179

Assistant patrol leader, 17

Assistant Senior patrol leader, 52

B

B-B-B-O-Y yell, 179

Baden-Powell patrol, 16; standards, 198

Ball over game, 152

Ball relay game, 156

Barber hand clap, 181

Be prepared skit, 184

Bible tableau skit idea, 185

Blanket-rolling game, 168

Blindfold compass walk, 105

Board of Review, 143

Bow saw relay, 121

Breakfast, 173, 175, 176

C

Cadences, hiking, 100

Camp, patrol in short term, 47; patrol in long term (summer camp), 48-49

Campfires, 116; rainy day, 117; ideas, 178-86

Camping, patrol, 106-19; equipment, 107; training, 107; planning, 108; taking off, 110; getting there, 111; menus, 112; activities, 114; safety, 114; campfires, 116; rainy day campfires, 117; clean up, 118-19

Camping skill award, 133

Cars, danger from, 97

Catch-on games, 181-83

Catsup bottle hand clap, 180

Cents of direction game, 161

Ceremonies, patrol, opening, 62; closing, 70

Chaplain aide, troop, 53

Cheermaster, patrol, 18

Chopper's relay game, 120

Chow mein dinner, 174

Circle out game, 149

Citizenship skill award, 128

"Clam" hand clap, 181

Coaching, patrol, 64-66

Committee work, patrol, 19

Communications games, 163-66

Communications skill award, 139

Community living skill award, 141

Compass and map games, 76-77

Compass games, 104-05, 157-61

Competitions, patrol, 19

Conservation skill award, 136

Cooking skill award, 134

Corner, patrol, 13

Cross-country hikes, 90

"Crossed and uncrossed" game, 182

Crossing the gap outdoor game, 167

Crows and cranes game, 151

D

Dehydration, danger from, 98

Den chief, 51

Den, patrol, 14

Dinner, 172, 174, 176

Direction finding, 105

Dodge ball game, 149

Do-this—Do-that game, 150

Dual games, 82

E

Environment skill award, 138

Equipment, camping, 107

F

Falls, danger from, 97
Family living skill award, 140
"Far-out" clove hitch game, 125
"Far-out" square knot game, 125
Fire-by-friction game, 123
Fire-making games, 122-23
First aid games, 75-76
First aid skill award, 130
Fitness games, 80-81, 148-57
Flag, patrol, 12; pole raising game, 169
Flip-a-coin hike, 96
Freak plant hunt game, 102
Freight train hand clap, 180
French toast breakfast, 173
Fried egg breakfast, 175
Fun and fitness games, 80-81
Fuzzy stick relay, 120

G

Games, patrol, 72-84; part in patrol meeting, 19
Games and Activities, Boy Scout, 169
Good turn, patrol, 20
Good turn yell, 179
Grubmaster, 18

H

Hand claps, 180
Heat exhaustion, 99
Heat stroke, 99
Hike and trail foods, 171
Hike dangers, 97-99; cars, 97; falls, 97; lightning, 97; wind-chill, 97; dehydration, 98; heat exhaustion, 99; heat stroke, 99
Hikemaster, 17
Hiking cadences, 100
Hiking, patrol, 84-105

Hiking, skill award, 131
Historical hikes, 95
Hot dog dinner, 176

I

Ideas for patrol meetings, 62-70; opening ceremonies, 62; coaching, 64-66; projects, 66; plans, 67; play, 68; closing ceremony, 70
Instructor, troop, 53

J

Jack's alive game, 182
Jump the shot game, 148
Junior assistant Scoutmaster, 52

K

Knot games, 72-74
Kung Fu master skit, 184

L

Lay out square game, 160
Leadership, 23-24
Leaf matching nature game, 102
Leaking backpack game, 166
Librarian, troop, 53
Lightning, 97
Locomotive cheer, 179
Logbook, patrol, 13
Lost, 92
Lunch, 173, 175, 177

M

Measure a distance game, 162
Measurement games, 162
Meetings, patrol, 19, 58-61
Membership, patrol, 16
Menus, 112, 170-177
Message relay game, 163
Mini orienteering, 105

Minute judging game, 162
"Mobilize" game, 103
Morse relay game, 165
Morse steal the bacon game, 165
Mystery hike, 95

N

Name sound-off hiking cadence, 100
Nature games, 102-103
Nature memory hunt game, 103
Nature scavenger hunt game, 102
Neckerchief slide, patrol, 13
"Now" recruiting hikes, 107
Number call game, 151

O

Observation and memory games, 78-79
Observation games, 166
Object Hunt game, 166
One-pitch softball game, 155
Over-hill, over-dale hiking cadences, 100
Order of the Arrow, 49-50

P

Pace off 50 meters game, 162
Pack relay game, 168
Pancake breakfast, 176
Parents, 33
Patrol, advancement, 20; camp games, 120-25; camp, short term, 47; camp, long term, 48-49, 120-25; corner, 193-94; flag, 187-91; food chest, 195-97; good turns, 20; hike games, 102-05; jobs, 17-18; idea tool chest, 147-99; leader's code, inside front cover; leaders' council, 21, 36-42; leader's job, 7; meetings, 19, 58-61; meeting games, 72-84; in troop, 35; in troop activities, 42-49; projects, 187-98; spirit, 10
Personal growth agreement conference, 143
Problem solving, 22

Q

Quartermaster, patrol, 17; troop, 52

R

"Rain" hand clap, 181
Rainy day campfires, 117
Ringleader game, 150
Roman chariot race, 124
Rope games, 124-25
Rubber ball relay game, 156

S

Safety, camping, 114; hiking, 97-99
Scout Law, games, 72; skit, 184; yell, 180
Scout spirit, 142
Scoutmaster, 54-57
Scribe, patrol, 17; troop, 52
Senior patrol leader, 52
Ship in the fog game, 157
Short skits, 183-85
Silent fun game, 164
Silver dollar hunt, 102
Singing, 178
Skill awards, 128-41
Skit bag, 185
Skit preparation, 183
Song, patrol, 13
Sound off hiking cadence, 100
Spaghetti dinner, 172
Spirit, patrol, 10, 16
Split the match game, 120
Stalking games, 166-67
Starburst compass game, 157-59

Steal the bacon game, 152
"Stiff" fitness game, 149
Storytelling, 186
String burning relay, 122
Summer camp, patrol in, 48-49
Swat 'em game, 150
Swimming skill award, 140

T

Talent show, 185
TV commercial skit, 184
Tent pitching game, 169
Treasurer, patrol 17
Three-legged soccer game, 154
This is the moon, 181
Tripod suspension game, 124
Troop historian, 53
Troop leaders, 50-57
Twenty questions game, 182

U

Under and over relay, 154
Uniform, 21

W

Walking statues game, 166
Wall chart, advancement, 198
"We are Boy Scouts" yell, 179
Wet weather fire building game,
    123
Why are you pulling that rope skit,
    184
Wind-chill, danger from, 97
Woods tools games, 120-21
Worst aid skit, 185

Y

Yell, patrol, 13
Yells, 178-79